SIX FIGURE FREEDOM

HOW HIGH EARNERS ARE ESCAPING THE SIX-FIGURE PARADOX BY ELIMINATING DEBT AND BUILDING WEALTH WITHOUT SACRIFICING THEIR LIFESTYLE

BEST SELLING AUTHOR
BRENNAN SCHLAGBAUM

ISBN: 979-8-9937324-0-4

First Edition

Visit: budgetdog.com

To Erin, who has always believed in me.

To Logan and Ellie, who remind me daily what actually matters.

And to every parent lying awake at night worrying about money - this book is proof that it gets better.

DOWNLOAD YOUR
FREE RESOURCES HERE

Throughout this book, you'll see references to free calculators and tools.

You can access all of them for free at:

sixfigurefreedombook.com/resources

TABLE OF CONTENTS

CHAPTER 4: YOUR THREE-STEP SYSTEM TO SIX-FIGURE FREEDOM...................47

CHAPTER 5: THE 3 STATEMENTS THAT WILL CHANGE EVERYTHING 65

CHAPTER 1:

THE SIX-FIGURE PARADOX

Here's something that might sound familiar...

You're scrolling through your bank account at 10pm at night, wondering where your six-figure salary actually went this month.

The mortgage got paid. The car payments cleared. But somehow, you're still living paycheck to paycheck.

If this hits close to home, take a breath. You're not imagining it, and you're definitely not alone.

A 2025 study revealed something that would shock most people: 52% of Americans earning over $100,000 annually report feeling financially stressed.[1] More than half of six-figure earners - people making more money than their parents ever dreamed of - are struggling financially.

Even more surprising? Research shows that 36% of people earning over $100,000 live paycheck to paycheck, unable to afford much beyond basic expenses.[2] We're talking about successful professionals, managers, and executives who should theoretically have their financial lives figured out.

And the problem is getting worse, not better. Between January 2023 and December 2024, delinquency rates among people earning $150,000 or more increased by 130%.[3]

Let me put that in perspective. You could be making more than 90% of American households and still be more likely to feel financially stressed than financially secure.

I've heard this story countless times. "I'm almost 40 years old, and certainly not where I need to be with things," one person told me recently. Another shared, "I make good money, but my 401k's turned off, and I haven't really been saving anything."

Maybe you're nodding along right now.

The truth is, you've stumbled into what I call the Six-Figure Paradox: the more you earn, the more complex your financial life becomes, and the further you seem to drift from the financial freedom you thought that salary would deliver.

This isn't your fault. The system that got you to six figures - working harder, earning more, upgrading your lifestyle - is the same system that's keeping you financially trapped.

But knowing you're trapped isn't enough. You need to see exactly who designed the trap... and why they specifically targeted people like you.

That's exactly what I discovered after years of living this problem myself and helping thousands of families escape it.

Here's What I Know About High-Earning Families Like Yours

Before I go any further, let me tell you why I'm qualified to help you with this.

My name is Brennan Schlagbaum. I'm a CPA who left my job at Deloitte after realizing my accounting expertise wasn't protecting me from the same financial mess every six-figure family faces.

Since then, I've worked with over 2,175 high-earning families through Budget Dog Academy, and the pattern is always the same: impressive salaries, mounting debt, and financial stress that no raise could fix.

I wasn't just observing this problem from the outside. I was also living it.

At age 23, my wife Erin and I sat down to assess our finances for the first time. The numbers were sobering: $76,000 in non-mortgage debt plus a $228,000 mortgage. We had $40,000 in student loans, $22,000 in car payments, $10,000 on an engagement ring I'd financed, and even $3,500 for a bed we'd bought on New Year's Eve because "we could afford the payments."

Despite having a solid career path at Deloitte and eventually earning my CPA, we were trapped in the same cycle I now see affecting thousands of high-earning professionals. We made good money, but we spent it faster than we earned it.

The wake-up call came when I realized we had accumulated over $304,000 in total debt. Here I was, a trained accountant who could audit million-dollar companies, but I couldn't manage my own family's finances.

That's when everything changed. Using the same step-by-step system I'd learned in corporate finance, I created a framework that eliminated our debt completely. We became millionaires by age 30, I left my corporate job, and we paid off our house in the same week.

But the real test came later. In 2022, our daughter Logan was diagnosed with Dravet syndrome, a rare form of epilepsy. She had 22 seizures that year. We lived in hospitals and emergency rooms while managing over $200,000 in medical bills.

During this crisis - the most stressful period of our lives - our financial system held. We not only survived, we grew our business by 10x while giving Logan the best care possible.

Since then, I've helped over 2,175 families save a collective $5.3 million using these same strategies. The average family saves $24,121, and they accelerate their debt payoff by 28 months.

That crisis forced me to create what I now call the Six-Figure Freedom Formula - a step-by-step system that eliminates financial chaos for high earners without sacrificing their lifestyle or requiring them to live like broke college students.

Unlike generic budgeting advice, this formula addresses the three core challenges every high earner faces: time scarcity, decision fatigue, and lifestyle preservation. It's the only system designed specifically for people earning $100K+ who want professional-grade results.

Here's what I wish someone had told me when I was drowning in that $304,000 of debt: every month you wait to fix this problem costs you more than just money.

I calculated it recently - if we hadn't turned things around when we did, we'd be sitting on over $500,000 in debt today. The compound interest alone would have cost us $196,000.

But the real cost? Logan's medical crisis would have bankrupted us. Instead of focusing on her care, I'd have been scrambling to refinance the house or begging family for loans.

Without a system, you're one economic downturn away from losing the lifestyle you've worked decades to build. The higher your income, the faster the fall.

I'm sharing this because I want you to understand something important: I've been exactly where you are. The shame, the frustration, the feeling that you should have this figured out by now - I've felt it all.

More importantly, I've found a way out. And I'm here to show you the same path.

But first, you need to understand why your intelligence might actually be working against you...

You're Not Broken, And You're Definitely Not Stupid

Let me guess what you're thinking right now.

Maybe it's something like, "How did I get here? I'm smart. I'm successful at work. I manage big budgets and lead teams. So why can't I figure out my own money?"

Your intelligence isn't the problem. In fact, it might be part of what got you into this situation.

There's something unique about high earners that most financial advice completely misses. The same drive and competence that made you successful in your career can actually work against you when it comes to personal finances.

Think about your typical workday. You're making 50+ decisions, solving complex problems, managing people and projects. By the time you get home, your brain is exhausted. The last thing you want to do is sit down and wrestle with budgets, investment accounts, and debt payoff strategies.

This isn't laziness. It's called decision fatigue, and research directly links this mental exhaustion to poorer financial choices

- excessive borrowing, delayed savings, and increased credit spending, especially among high-pressure professionals.

You see this every day without realizing it. Automatically saying yes to the premium car wash. Upgrading flights without comparing prices. Choosing the most expensive option because 'good enough' feels like settling.

These aren't character flaws - they're predictable responses to being mentally exhausted.

The numbers back this up. Consumer debt has reached $1.21 trillion according to the Federal Reserve's 2025 data, with rising late-payment rates.[4]

Studies show that the demanding mental pressure of professional work reduce self-control, leading to exactly these kinds of impulsive financial behaviors.

So every month you delay costs more than just interest - it costs you missed chances to save money, tax inefficiencies, and compound growth working against you instead of for you.

While you're dealing with decision fatigue, society expects you to have it all figured out. After all, you make good money, right? You must be financially secure.

The shame that comes with this assumption is real and isolating. Only 38% of people feel comfortable discussing their finances.[5] and that number drops even lower for high earners. When you're supposed to be "successful," admitting financial struggles feels like admitting failure.

And money stress doesn't stay at work. It follows you home. It creates tension with your spouse.

Your children absorb the anxiety even when you try to hide it, learning that money is something to worry about rather than a tool for freedom.

A friend I spoke to recently put it perfectly: "I don't want to think about money so much. I just want to live my life, have fun with my family, and know that everything's set up so I can enjoy life."

That's not too much to ask. And it's exactly what this book will help you achieve because I've done it myself, and I've helped thousands of other families just like you.

This book IS that different approach - one designed specifically for people in your situation.

But first, you need to see where your money is actually disappearing...

The Money Leaks You Can't See Coming

Let me show you where your money is actually going. It's probably not what you think.

Most high earners focus on the big expenses - the mortgage, car payments, maybe that vacation to Europe. But the *real* damage happens in the margins, through what I call "invisible money drains."

Healthcare costs alone are rising 5-7% annually according to Springbok Wealth's 2025 analysis. And Bankrate's 2025 Emergency Savings Report shows that 59% of Americans can't even cover a $1,000 emergency.[7]

Your insurance premiums are quietly eating more of your paycheck each year as well. A Morning Consult 2025 study found that emergency expenses have jumped 29% in just two years - the median unexpected cost is now $585, up from $455 in 2023.[8]

Then there's subscription creep. You sign up for Netflix, then add Spotify, then Apple TV, then that meal kit delivery service, then the premium version of that app you use once a month.

They seem small at the time, but it's 'death by a thousand cuts'. Before you know it, you're spending hundreds monthly on services you barely use.

But the biggest drain? The 'lifestyle upgrade'.

A 2024 AdvisorFinder survey found that people earning over $100K often fall into what Forbes describes as the lifestyle inflation trap.[2]

You get a raise, so you reward yourself. Bigger house, nicer car, better vacation. Each upgrade feels justified because now you can "afford" the payments.

What happens is the 'breathing space' you just received is now being traded for bigger and better things, leaving you at breakeven again when the bills come in.

This is what I call the status trap. Your peers upgraded their lifestyle, so you feel obligated to match it. The higher your income, the higher the expectations to "look successful." You justify debt with future income, but future income creates future expenses.

The Resolution Foundation's 2025 Living Standards Outlook shows that mortgage costs are inflating faster than wages, squeezing budgets even for high earners.[9] What used to be a manageable housing payment becomes a financial anchor when combined with all the other upgraded expenses.

A parent I was talking to the other day told me, "I'm not going to say no to my kids, you know. My son's sports, the gym membership, the landscaping service - yes, I could cut those, but weekends are for spending time with my kids, not mowing the lawn."

That's fair. There's nothing more important than time with the family, and every single one of those choices makes sense in isolation.

But together, they create a web of expenses that trap you in a cycle where more income never feels like enough.

The real danger isn't just the monthly drain. It's what happens when life hits hard - and it always does.

Last year, I watched a successful attorney - someone making $240,000 annually - lose his job during company restructuring. Within four months, he was behind on his mortgage.

The landscaping service, private school tuition, and car payments that seemed so reasonable when the pay checks were coming? They became financial quicksand.

He had to pull his kids from their school, sell the house at a loss, and move in with his in-laws. All because he couldn't cut $8,000 in monthly fixed expenses fast enough to match his unemployment benefits.

With all these fixed expenses, any income disruption becomes catastrophic. The higher your lifestyle costs, the more vulnerable you become.

But there's something even more insidious than lifestyle inflation that's draining your wealth - something that makes intelligent people like you more financially fragile than you ever imagined...

The Success Trap That's Keeping You Stuck

You've worked hard to get where you are. Your skills got you promoted. Your expertise made you valuable. Your income puts you in the top 10% of earners in America. Financially, you should feel like you're winning.

So why does it feel like you're more financially vulnerable now than when you were making half as much?

There's a cruel irony at play. The same lifestyle that signals your professional success is actually making you more fragile, not stronger.

When you were making $50,000, you lived in a smaller place, drove an older car, ate out less often. If something happened to your job, you could cut expenses quickly and survive on savings or a lower-paying position.

Now? Your fixed costs have scaled with your income. The bigger mortgage, the car payments, the private school tuition, the family vacations that everyone expects. These aren't just expenses anymore - they're commitments that don't disappear when times get tough.

If unemployment hit now, your $150K self has maybe three weeks before missing the mortgage payment. The higher you climb, the faster you fall when the income stops.

And the professional landscape is shifting in ways that make this lifestyle trap even more dangerous.

Many careers that built the modern six-figure middle class are facing major changes.

Forbes reports that everyone from financial analysts to bookkeepers, paralegals, and contract lawyers face significant risk from AI systems that can rapidly process data sets, draft contracts, and conduct routine reviews.[10]

By 2030, it's projected that 30% of current jobs (nearly 1 in 3 workers) will be impacted by AI automation according to The Resume Genius 2025 report.[11]

The jobs most at risk? Those involving "repetitive analysis, data processing, and routine legal or administrative tasks" - exactly the kind of work that many high earners do.

Your six-figure salary won't protect you from the next inevitable economic downturn if you're carrying massive debt and high fixed expenses.

High earners with lifestyle inflation are statistically more likely to lose their homes during economic downturns because their fixed costs can't be reduced quickly enough to match reduced income.

This isn't about fear though - it's about preparation. The research shows the pattern clearly: 73% of employees can barely afford expenses beyond basic living costs,[1] and emergency expenses have jumped 29% in just two years.[6] Higher income doesn't create security when it's matched by higher fixed costs.

The families who weather financial storms aren't the ones with the highest incomes. They're the ones with the lowest fixed costs relative to their earnings.

Most high earners are one major crisis away from financial catastrophe despite their income - medical emergencies, job loss, or family crises can destroy decades of lifestyle building within months when debt-to-income ratios are high and emergency funds are minimal.

And that's exactly what most financial advice gets backwards about high earners...

Why This Book Isn't Like Anything Else You've Tried

You've probably heard promises like this before.

Maybe you've bought other financial books, downloaded budgeting apps, or tried following advice from finance gurus who've never lived in your situation.

Unfortunately, most financial advice treats everyone the same: cut your expenses, make a budget, pay off debt, start investing (as if a family making $150,000 has the same challenges as someone making $40,000).

They don't.

High earners need different strategies, different tools, and different approaches. You can't use college-student budgeting advice when you're managing a mortgage, childcare, aging parents, and career demands all at the same time.

This book was built specifically for people in your situation. Not just because I've studied high-earner finances professionally, but because I've lived it personally as well.

I understand the pressure to maintain a certain lifestyle. I know what it's like to have "good" debt and "necessary" expenses that somehow add up to financial stress. I've felt the embarrassment of making great money but having nothing to show for it.

More importantly, I've found a way out. And so have the 2,175+ families who've used these same strategies through Budget Dog

Academy, collectively saving over $5.3 million in their first year alone and putting them on the road to real, sustainable wealth.

As a CPA who lived through this exact struggle, I understand both the professional success that got you here and the personal financial chaos that's keeping you stuck.

The Six-Figure Freedom Formula bridges that gap.

Hand on heart, I can say that this system works differently than anything you've ever tried before.

Instead of restriction and deprivation, it's built on automation and optimization. Instead of generic advice, it's designed around the specific challenges that high earners face.

You won't find lectures about skipping lattes or cutting cable. You'll find professional-grade strategies adapted for busy, successful people who want their financial life to work as well as their career does.

As one parent told me recently, "I just know what I'm doing is not working. I mean, I have a budget spreadsheet, but I just really don't have a plan in place."

That's exactly what we're going to build together.

Over the next ten chapters, you'll discover the same 3-step framework that has helped 2,175+ families transform financial chaos into a system that eliminates 50+ daily money decisions so you can focus on what matters.

You'll learn why your intelligence has been working against you, how to set up systems that run themselves, and how to protect everything you build.

Most importantly, you'll finally understand that you're not the problem, it's the approach you've been using that is the problem.

Let's get to work and fix that.

But before we dive into the solution, I need to show you something that will probably make you uncomfortable.

In Chapter 2, you'll discover the specific psychological trap that's even more dangerous than lifestyle inflation - one that's hardwired into high achievers and is probably influencing your money decisions right now without you realizing it.

It's the reason why the smartest people often make the dumbest financial mistakes. And once you see it, you'll never fall for it again.

CHAPTER 2:

SMART MONEY, NOT-SO-SMART DECISIONS

"I make good money, and yet I cannot keep up with expenses."

This came from an anaesthetist earning over $200,000 annually. Despite her impressive income, she felt completely out of control financially. She's not alone in this struggle.

The UBS 2024 Investor Survey revealed something troubling: 62% of high-income professionals overestimate their personal financial skills[1]. These are people who can manage multi-million dollar budgets at work but somehow struggle with their own monthly expenses.

This disconnect shows up constantly in the families I work with. Successful professionals who excel at complex workplace decisions feel completely lost when it comes to their own money.

Why Brilliant Professionals Struggle With Money

Here's what most people don't understand: being smart at work can actually hurt you when it comes to your personal finances.

A CFO who handles billions at work has $67,000 in credit card debt. A project manager running $50 million projects can't explain where her high six-figure salary goes. A business consultant has never checked the investment fees costing him $4,200 a year.

These aren't dumb people. The problem is that work money and personal money need different skills.

At work, you have help. Teams handle different tasks. Someone else makes the budget. Another person tracks the spending. You follow company rules and systems that already exist.

At home? It's just you. After a long day of making decisions, you're supposed to figure out investments. Research retirement accounts. Track every expense. All by yourself, when you're already tired.

The same confidence that helps you at work becomes a problem at home. You assume that since you're good with company money, you should be good with your own money. But they're not the same thing.

One woman told us her story. "I analyze data for a living, but I don't know where my money goes." She spent eight hours a day making reports at work. Meanwhile, her $115,000 salary was draining away. She had fifteen subscriptions she'd forgotten about.

This happens to lots of smart people. Six-figure families often lose tens of thousands each year without realizing it. The money just disappears through cracks they can't see.

But there's a reason smart people struggle with money, and once you understand why, everything gets easier.

Your Brain Shuts Down At Exactly The Wrong Time

That specific reason? Your decision-making energy has a daily limit - and you hit it long before you get home.

Think about yesterday. By 10 AM, you'd already chosen which emails to prioritize, decided how to handle that difficult client, and figured out the approach for your afternoon presentation.

By lunch, you'd made 50+ micro-decisions that all needed mental energy.

Here's how this shows up in your life: You come home mentally drained and automatically say yes to premium grocery delivery (there goes $30).

You renew that software subscription without checking if you still use it (another $200).

You stick with expensive investment accounts because researching alternatives feels impossible when your brain is fried.

One Academy member told me she'd been paralyzed for over a year, unable to choose between paying debt or starting her retirement investments - second-guessing every decision and ending up doing nothing.

The Federal Reserve's latest data shows consumer debt hitting $5.06 trillion with rising late-payment rates[2]. Work pressure wears down your self-control. That's when you make impulse purchases and put off money planning.

Your brain can only make so many good decisions each day. After using them all at work, you have nothing left for money choices that could save you thousands.

But you can set up your money to run without you. No daily decisions needed, and in the next chapter I'll show you how.

The Hidden Drain That Costs More Than Your Mortgage

When your brain is tired from work, putting off money decisions costs you more and more.

Here's the math that will shock you: that subscription you've been meaning to cancel? It's not just $50 monthly - it's $600 annually, plus the $180 in compound interest you could have earned investing that money.

The expensive investment account you never switched over? It's not just the high fees - it's costing you $4,200 yearly in unnecessary charges, plus $126,000 over twenty years in lost compound growth.

These aren't small problems. They're big money drains that get worse the more you earn.

One project manager earning $180,000 told us: "When a hard day comes, I feel that I deserve to spend money." After brutal days managing competing deadlines, that $200 dinner feels earned. The $800 weekend trip feels necessary. Each choice makes perfect sense when you're mentally spent.

But here's what is brutal about earning six figures: you will lose more of your income when you're tired than someone else on a lower income who also overspends.

Someone making $40,000 might overspend by $100 a month, but with your income, you might overspend by $1,000. Same exhaustion, ten times the damage.

Add it up over ten years and you've lost $347,000. Over twenty years, it's almost a million dollars lost when you factor in missed investment returns.

That's enough to buy a house in cash. Or retire five years early. Or fund your children's entire college education. Instead, it evaporates through hundreds of tired choices that each seemed reasonable at the moment.

The key lies in understanding how to structure your financial systems to work with your psychology instead of against it.

The Automation Trap That's Bleeding You Dry

Automation is powerful for your money - when done right. High-earning families who consistently build wealth use automation all the time. But there's a big difference between smart automation and lazy automation.

Smart automation includes regular reviews. You set up systems, then check them monthly to improve performance. Lazy automation is "set it and forget it" - you never look again.

I've seen this firsthand when people first arrive in the Academy. A director earning high six-figures had automated his investments three years earlier, then never reviewed them. Those high-fee accounts were costing him $4,200 yearly - money that could have funded the family vacation he kept saying   they couldn't afford.

Here's the trap: you automate to save mental energy, which is smart. But then you never update or improve those systems, which bleeds money. You're automatically investing $500 monthly in expensive funds when low-cost alternatives exist. Your insurance auto-renews at higher rates yearly because you never shop around.

One family was automatically investing $800 monthly while carrying $22,000 in credit card debt at 24% interest. They had the right automation instinct but the wrong priority order. The mental relief of "at least I'm saving" was costing them $3,400 annually in net interest.

"We don't have a budget or a sense of where our money goes," one engineer earning $100,000 told us. He had automated bill pay and investments but no oversight system to ensure they were actually helping him build wealth.

The solution isn't avoiding automation - it's automating with intelligence. Set up your systems, then review them monthly.

There's a specific sequence for setting up these automated systems that determines whether they build or bleed wealth, but I don't want to get ahead of myself – that's coming up!

The Shame Spiral That Costs Six Figures

Money is the one topic nobody discusses honestly - not even with close friends. For high earners, this silence becomes financial quicksand.

Think about your last networking event. Colleagues freely shared career wins, project challenges, even relationship struggles. But when someone mentioned their "expensive mortgage payment," the conversation shifted immediately. Nobody admits they're drowning in debt when they're supposed to look successful.

The Wells Fargo 2024 study found just 36% of people earning $150,000 or more feel comfortable discussing their financial situation openly.[3] This number drops even lower for executives.

The higher your income, the more society expects you to have money figured out. This creates a vicious cycle: you can't ask for help because that might signal professional incompetence.

One company director earning $140,000 told us, "I feel like my partner and I aren't on the same page. Money talks turn tense, so we avoid them." Even married couples struggle with honest financial conversations when both people feel they should already know what to do.

Here's what makes this particularly brutal for high earners: the shame prevents you from getting help that could save you thousands annually. You research investment strategies in secret. You worry about debt while pretending everything is fine. You suffer through financial confusion because admitting you need help feels like professional failure.

Meanwhile, someone making $40,000 gets sympathy and support for money struggles. Nobody judges them for needing financial help. But when you earn six figures and still feel financially lost? The judgment feels crushing, even when it's mostly in your head.

The isolation makes every financial problem worse. You're trying to solve difficult money issues during the few hours when your brain isn't already tired from work decisions. One director earning north of $180,000 wrote to us feeling embarrassed about basic tax confusion despite his professional success.

What successful families discovered was that financial shame doesn't just create isolation - it creates expensive behavioral patterns that drain your wealth in predictable ways.

Work Stress Becomes Shopping Therapy

Your brain creates a dangerous equation: hard work = earned reward. After endless days managing competing deadlines, that $200 dinner doesn't feel like overspending. It feels like a reward you've earned.

"When a hard day or hard season comes, I feel that I am entitled to spend," one actuary earning $180,000 told us. This captures the reward mentality that traps high earners in a vicious cycle.

The PNC 2024 study found 45% of Americans say their spending often goes over budget due to stress or emotional triggers.[4] But here's where it becomes difficult when you're earning six figures: your stress purchases aren't $20 impulse buys. They're flight upgrades, premium services, and expensive social activities because "we can afford it."

Think about your last stressful week. You probably made several micro-rewards without conscious thought. Premium grocery delivery instead of regular. The expensive restaurant instead of cooking. The weekend trip because you "needed" to decompress.

Each choice makes perfect sense when you're mentally exhausted. The temporary relief even reinforces the pattern.

Work pressure leads to reward purchases. The brief dopamine hit makes stress spending feel like effective self-care.

PNC's research showed 51% of people make "retail therapy" purchases more than once a month.[4] But when you earn six figures, retail therapy costs hundreds, not dollars. One client was spending an extra $800 monthly through stress purchases she didn't even track.

The pattern becomes automatic: Bad day at work → "I deserve this" → Purchase → Brief relief → Return to stress → Bigger purchase next time. Soon you're spending hundreds extra monthly without realizing it because each individual choice felt justified.

You already manage reward systems effectively at work - bonuses, recognition, team incentives. That same strategic thinking can redesign your personal reward system to build wealth instead of draining it.

When Your Worth Gets Tied To Your Wealth

Your investment account balance affects how you feel about yourself more than you realize. When those numbers drop, it's not just financial concern - it feels like personal failure.

"I'm the spender and I tend to impulse buy in the moment," one chiropractor told us. The guilt from overspending creates a difficult cycle: spend impulsively, feel bad about yourself, avoid dealing with money, spend more to feel better.

Kansas State University's 2024 research explains this - and it shocked me when I first read it. They found 67% of people earning $125,000 or more report that their net worth heavily influenced their self-esteem.[6] The more professionally successful you become, the more your identity becomes tied to financial performance.

This creates a psychological trap unique to high earners (unfortunately I've seen this more times than I'd like to admit). You start believing your financial situation reflects your personal value. A bad investment month makes you feel incompetent. Debt makes you feel ashamed, even when it's from reasonable choices like buying a house.

And what makes this particularly damaging is when your self-worth depends on your net worth, every financial decision becomes emotionally charged. You avoid looking at accounts when they're down. You delay financial planning because the numbers feel like a judgment on your character.

One family had avoided checking their investment accounts for eight months because the market downturn made them feel like "financial failures." They were missing rebalancing opportunities that cost them $3,200 in potential returns.

The research shows high earners often compare their financial progress to their career progress. You got promoted, so your investments should be performing well too. When reality doesn't match expectations, the disappointment hits harder because it feels personal.

Think about the last time your net worth dropped. Did you feel a little sick to your stomach? Not just worried about the money, but like you'd somehow failed personally? That's your identity getting tangled up with your financial outcomes.

You already separate your professional performance from your personal   worth - you know a bad quarter doesn't make you a bad person. The same emotional intelligence that serves you at work can protect your financial decision-making.

Why A Little Knowledge Can Be Dangerous

You probably know more about money than most people. You understand compound interest. You've heard of index funds. You know debt is generally bad and saving is generally good.

But the trap is that knowing the basics can make you overconfident about the details.

This is called the Dunning-Kruger effect. People with limited knowledge in a subject often overestimate their competence. In money management, a little knowledge can be dangerous because it makes you think you don't need help with the complicated stuff.

You read a few investment articles and feel confident picking individual stocks. You understand mortgage basics and skip shopping around for better rates. You know budgeting is important but figure you can wing it without a systematic approach.

"I lose track of where the small subscriptions, the $20, $40 here and there go," one client earning $130,000 told us. She understood big-picture financial concepts but was missing the small details that turned out to be draining her of thousands annually.

This false confidence prevents you from seeking the professional-grade systems that high earners actually need. You assume your general intelligence will handle the specifics. Meanwhile, you're losing money through inefficiencies you don't even see.

The most dangerous part? You don't know what you don't know. Tax optimization strategies that could save you $5,000 annually. Investment account structures that could reduce fees by thousands. Insurance coverage gaps that could cost you everything in a crisis.

Successful people in other fields rely on experts and systems. You wouldn't do your own legal work or medical procedures. But with money, the combination of basic knowledge and professional confidence tricks you into thinking you've got it handled.

The same analytical skills that made you successful professionally are exactly what you need to master this. You already know how to evaluate systems and implement processes. You just need the right financial framework to apply those skills to.

The Pressure To Look Successful

When you earn six figures, you move into social circles where everyone expects you to look the part. Your colleagues drive nice cars. Your neighbors have beautiful homes. Your friends take amazing vacations and post about them on social media.

Even when you don't care about status, the peer pressure is real. When everyone around you upgrades, staying still feels like moving backwards.

"Lifestyle creep... as I have received promotions, we seem to spend more," one company director told us. "The spending isn't necessarily on things as it is more so on the convenience and frequency of eating out."

It wasn't about buying luxury items. It was about matching the lifestyle expectations of her peer group.

This pressure operates differently than regular peer pressure — there's nobody telling you directly to "upgrade your lifestyle." Instead, it happens through a thousand small social cues. The restaurant your colleagues choose for lunch. The hotels they book for business trips. The neighborhoods they live in.

You start to feel awkward suggesting cheaper alternatives. When everyone else orders the expensive wine, you do too. When your peer group talks about their cleaning services, you hire one. When they mention private schools, you start researching options.

Each decision seems reasonable in isolation. But together, they create a lifestyle inflation that keeps pace with your income growth. You earn more, you spend more, and you never actually get ahead financially.

The psychology is subtle but powerful (and honestly, most people don't even realize it's happening). You're not trying to show off. You're trying to fit in. You don't want to seem cheap or unsuccessful in front of people whose respect you value professionally.

This is why high earners often feel financially stretched despite substantial incomes. Your lifestyle expenses grow to match your peer group's expectations, leaving little room for actual wealth building.

But here's what's encouraging about this pattern - it's entirely manageable with the right approach. You already handle tricky work relationships and manage what your boss expects. Those same people skills can handle social pressure while you redirect your money toward building wealth instead of looking wealthy.

How All These Problems Feed Each Other

Now that you understand the psychological patterns that trap high earners, let me show you how they all connect, because unfortunately, each problem we've talked about makes the others worse. They don't exist separately - they create a cycle that keeps you stuck.

So picture this: You're tired from making so many decisions at work, so you make lazy money choices when you get home. That spending creates money stress.

The money stress makes you feel bad about yourself. But feeling bad about your money makes you avoid dealing with it, so you don't check your accounts. You don't fix problems. You don't talk honestly with your spouse about money.

Meanwhile, the money problems get worse. More debt. Higher fees. Missed chances to save. The stress builds up and you spend money to feel better - that expensive dinner, the weekend trip, the upgrade you didn't need.

The quick relief makes the pattern stronger. Work stress leads to spending. Spending creates shame. Shame leads to avoiding money stuff. Avoiding problems makes them worse. Worse problems create more stress.

"I just know what I'm doing is not working," one client told us. She felt stuck in a loop where money problems created emotional problems, which created more money problems.

Here's what's important to understand (and this took me years to figure out): recognizing these patterns puts you ahead of most high earners who never   see the connections. You already know how to spot problems and fix systems at work - the same skills that built your career can rebuild your financial foundation.

These patterns can be broken. You don't need more willpower. You need the right systems that work even when you're tired, stressed, or upset.

The solution lies in understanding exactly how these cycles operate and the specific points that break them.

Why The Six-Figure Freedom Formula Works Differently

Most financial advice assumes you have unlimited time and energy to make smart money decisions every day. It treats a $40,000 earner the same as a $150,000 earner. It expects you to track every expense, research every investment, and optimize every choice.

The Six-Figure Freedom Formula works differently because it's built around how high earners actually live and think.

Traditional budgeting requires constant willpower. The Formula uses automation so your money works even when you're exhausted from work decisions.

Other systems demand daily tracking. The Formula needs just 30 minutes monthly because everything runs automatically.

Generic financial advice ignores the psychological barriers we've discussed. The Formula eliminates them. Instead of fighting decision fatigue, it removes most financial decisions from your daily routine. Instead of relying on discipline, it creates systems that work regardless of your emotional state.

Most financial systems fail during life's inevitable crises. The Formula was literally tested during my daughter's medical emergency when we faced over $200,000 in medical bills.

Not only did it hold, but the systems we'd built kept running automatically while we lived in the hospital, proving that the right financial foundation can withstand even the worst storms.

The 2,175 families who've transformed their finances using this Formula didn't develop superhuman willpower. They stopped fighting their psychology and started working with it. The Formula treats your family finances with the same systematic approach you use at work - monthly strategic reviews, not daily panic and guesswork.

Now that you understand why your intelligence has been working against you, let me show you how the Six-Figure Freedom Formula turns those same analytical skills into your greatest financial asset.

CHAPTER 3:

THE 30-MINUTE PROMISE: HOW YOU FINALLY TAKE CONTROL

Recently, a high-earning client discovered she was losing hundreds each month through what I call 'invisible bleeds' – subscription creep, forgotten insurance riders, and investment fees she never knew existed.

That doesn't sound like a lot, but it's over $10,000 annually – slipping away from someone who thought she had her finances handled.

When we analyzed 2,175 families in Budget Dog Academy, we found high earners commonly lose thousands each year through money leaks they can't even see.

You could spend months trying to plug these leaks one by one. Or you could do what actually works: build a system that eliminates them entirely in 30 minutes per month.

That's what this chapter is about. The 30-minute promise that finally puts you in control of your money without fighting your psychology every step of the way.

I know what you're thinking. You've heard promises like this before. You've tried systems that seemed simple at first but became overwhelming when life got busy.

Maybe you downloaded budget apps that felt motivating for a week before you stopped using them. Or built detailed spreadsheets that looked professional but became impossible to maintain during hectic periods.

The Pew Research Center found that only 34% of people who download budget apps use them beyond the first month.[1] These systems simply weren't designed for people with your income level and time constraints.

You need something different. Not another system that requires daily attention you don't have. Not another budget that assumes you want to spend evenings tracking coffee purchases instead of helping with homework.

Let me show you what continuing without a system actually costs.

Imagine Michael, a software architect making around $165,000. Without a clear system, he spends 3–4 hours a week juggling seven different apps. That's 200 hours a year—five workweeks—lost to busywork. The real cost? Missing moments with the people who matter most.

But the real cost? He missed his daughter's soccer championship because he was home reconciling accounts. He turned down a startup opportunity because he couldn't quickly assess if he could handle the salary cut. The invisible costs compound faster than any interest rate.

You need a system that works with your schedule, not against it. One that reduces financial decisions instead of creating more. One that takes 30 minutes monthly, not 30 minutes daily.

That's exactly what the Six-Figure Freedom Formula delivers. And in this chapter, I'll show you how it transforms financial chaos into automated clarity without requiring you to change who you are or how you live.

Let's start with why every system you've tried before was designed to fail.

The 30-Minute Promise That Will Fix Your Financial Chaos

Here's what makes the Six-Figure Freedom Formula different from every other financial system you've tried: it takes 30 minutes *monthly*, not daily work you have to keep up with.

Most financial advice assumes you have tons of time for money management. Track every expense. Check your budget weekly. Research investments constantly. Make dozens of money decisions each month.

But here's what research shows. The Consumer Financial Protection Bureau studied this. Tools that need more than one hour per week? People quit using them 70% more often. Tools that need less than one hour per month? People stick with them.[2]

Your brain already knows this. Systems that work long-term need very little daily effort.

The 30-minute promise isn't about doing less work. It's about building a system so good that it runs itself between monthly check-ins.

Think about how you handle big projects at work. You don't check every detail every day. You set up systems. You delegate tasks. You do monthly reviews to make sure everything stays on track. The Six-Figure Freedom Formula uses this same approach for your money.

Parents tell us the same thing again and again—they want breathing room, not a second job. That's what 30 minutes monthly gives you. Complete control of your money without making it another career.

Here's what happens in those 30 minutes. You look at three simple reports that show where you stand. You make any changes needed. You check that everything runs automatically. Done.

No daily expense tracking. No weekly budget meetings. No constant money decisions eating up your thinking time.

Gallup studied people with automated money systems and found they have 42% less financial stress on Sunday nights compared to people who manage money manually.[3] That's the difference between dreading Monday morning and knowing everything is handled.

But automation without checking becomes the "set it and forget it" trap from Chapter 2. The Six-Figure Freedom Formula prevents this through smart monthly reviews that keep your system working without taking over your life.

This approach respects both your money and your time - because at your income level, time is your scarcest resource.

You Don't Need To Sacrifice What You've Worked For

Here's what you won't have to do with the Six-Figure Freedom Formula: cut your children's activities, cancel family vacations, or move to a smaller house.

Most financial advice assumes you need to make big cuts to get ahead. Skip the coffee. Cancel subscriptions. Live like you're broke until you're rich.

That approach might work for someone making $40,000. But when you're earning six figures, the math is different. You're not spending too much on the big things. You're losing money through systems that don't work well.

High earners don't want to sacrifice what they've worked for - the good schools, the family vacations, the home they love. They want to make their money work better, not cut the things that matter to their families.

The Six-Figure Freedom Formula does exactly that. It finds the money leaks you can't see and puts that cash toward building wealth. No lifestyle changes needed.

Think about it this way. You're already earning enough money to be wealthy. It's just disappearing through broken systems instead of working for you.

Families often find they're losing thousands each year to investment fees they didn't even know they were paying. Others find they're wasting thousands a year on subscriptions they forgot they had. Some families save thousands just by switching insurance companies without changing their coverage.

None of these families changed how they lived. They just fixed the leaks.

The Formula works by making things work better, not cutting things out. You keep living the life you've built. Your money just starts working harder.

This is why the Formula works for high earners specifically. You've worked hard to reach your income level. You've earned the right to enjoy it. The last thing you want is a financial system that makes you feel guilty about every purchase.

The Formula respects both your smarts and your lifestyle. It assumes you want to build wealth without feeling deprived. It assumes you want your children to keep their activities and your family to keep taking vacations.

Most importantly, it assumes you're smart enough to tell the difference between making your money work better and restricting your life.

That's exactly the kind of system you're about to build.

Your Complete Financial Picture In One Place

Right now, your money is probably scattered everywhere.

You have to log into five different websites just to figure out where you stand. Checking account here, savings there, investment accounts somewhere else. Credit cards with different companies. Maybe a 401k you haven't looked at in months.

When you want to know if you can afford something, you end up playing detective across multiple apps and statements just to get a basic picture.

This is the opposite of how you probably operate. Think about your work dashboard. You probably track KPIs, project milestones, and team metrics in one unified view.

You'd never run a project checking seven different systems for basic status updates. But that's exactly how most high earners run their personal finances - like a project manager working without a dashboard.

The J.D. Power Digital Banking study found that 41% of high earners quit using financial tools because "information was spread across too many screens."[4] They want one place to see everything that matters.

The Six-Figure Freedom Formula gives you exactly that. One screen that shows your complete financial picture in under 30 seconds.

No more logging into multiple accounts to figure out if you can afford something. No more guessing whether you're ahead or behind this month. No more wondering if your automated systems are actually working.

Clients often say they want a simple, one-screen system that makes it easy to see everything in one place. That's exactly what the Formula delivers.

Here's what you see on that one screen - income coming in, expenses going out, debt remaining, wealth building, and whether you're on track or need adjustments.

Everything important. Nothing extra. Updated automatically.

This isn't about having fancy software or expensive apps. It's about designing a system so clear that you always know exactly where you stand.

Think about how this changes your daily life. No more second-guessing purchases because you're not sure what you can afford. No more Sunday night stress wondering if you have enough money for next week's expenses.

Just clarity. And confidence. And the peace of mind that comes from knowing your money situation at all times.

That one-screen view becomes the foundation for everything else the Formula does. Because you can't make your money work better if you can't see what's happening clearly.

The End Of Financial Anxiety

If you're anything like me, Sunday night used to mean financial anxiety. I'd lie in bed wondering if I had enough money for the week ahead. Should I check my account balance or just hope for the best? Did that automatic payment go through? Can I afford groceries and gas this week?

Monday morning brought more stress. Opening my banking app with one eye closed, hoping the numbers weren't as bad as I feared.

But here's what changes when you implement the Six-Figure Freedom Formula. Sunday nights look completely different. You already know exactly where you stand. Your system updated automatically throughout the week. Your one-screen view showed you the truth all month long.

No surprises. No anxiety. No hoping your account has enough money.

Instead, you're thinking about weekend plans with the kids. You're planning next week's projects at work. You're focused on things that actually matter to your life and your family.

Monday morning becomes routine instead of stressful. You check your one screen for 30 seconds, see that everything is running smoothly, and move on with your day.

Think about how much mental energy you currently spend on money worries. Wondering if you can afford things. Stressing about bills. Avoiding financial conversations with your spouse because they're too overwhelming.

Many high earners say that by the end of the month, they look at what's left—and there's nothing there. That constant drain means daily stress and endless worry.

All that energy gets freed up when your system works automatically. You can focus on your career growth, your family time, your personal interests. The things you actually care about.

This isn't about ignoring your money. It's about setting up systems that work so well you don't have to think about them constantly.

Your money becomes like electricity in your house. It works in the background, powering everything you want to do, without requiring daily management or worry.

That's the kind of financial peace the Six-Figure Freedom Formula creates.

The Only Framework You'll Ever Need

Now you understand what the Six-Figure Freedom Formula can do for you. Thirty minutes monthly instead of daily stress. Your lifestyle stays the same while you build wealth. One screen that shows everything you need to know. The end of Sunday night money worry.

Now you're probably wondering: how does this actually work?

The answer is a step-by-step plan that's completely different from anything you've tried before. Most money advice tries to fix your problems one piece at a time. Pay off debt first, then save, then invest. Or save first, then worry about debt later.

That one-piece-at-a-time method is exactly why you've felt stuck. You can't fix one part of your money while the other parts keep bleeding cash. You need all the pieces working together from day one.

The Six-Figure Freedom Formula does exactly that. It's a complete system that handles everything at the same time. No more choosing between different money goals. No more wondering if you're focusing on the right thing.

This isn't about learning complicated money theories or becoming an investment expert. It's about following a plan that works. Over 2,175 families have already used it to save more than $5.3 million combined. Those kinds of savings are enough for a family vacation or three months of college.

The families who changed their money lives didn't need superhuman willpower. They didn't need to become money geniuses. They just needed to follow clear steps designed for high earners.

That's what makes this different from every other approach you've tried. It's not another budget method or investment strategy. It's a complete money system built around how you actually live and work.

You already have the smarts and skills to make this work. You just need the right plan to use them.

The Six-Figure Freedom Formula works because it's designed around how high earners actually think and live.

But here's what nobody tells you about financial systems: the first step isn't what you'd expect. It has nothing to do with budgets, spreadsheets, or cutting expenses.

It starts with something I discovered during my daughter's medical crisis - when our finances had to work perfectly while we lived in the hospital. The same principle that kept us afloat during 22 seizures and endless medical bills is what makes the entire system bulletproof.

In Chapter 4, I'll show you exactly what that principle is and why it changes everything about how you'll manage money.

CHAPTER 4:

YOUR THREE-STEP SYSTEM TO SIX-FIGURE FREEDOM

You might remember from Chapter 1 that in 2022, my daughter Logan was diagnosed with Dravet syndrome - a rare form of epilepsy that would test everything about our financial system.

When she was having her third seizure in 48 hours, I wasn't thinking about budgets. I was watching monitors, talking to doctors, trying to understand words like "Dravet syndrome" and "refractory epilepsy."

But our money kept working.

While we lived in that hospital - and I mean literally lived there, sleeping in chairs, eating vending machine dinners - every bill got paid. Every investment contribution happened. Our automated systems never missed a beat.

That's when I knew the Six-Figure Freedom Formula wasn't just theory. It worked when life fell apart.

The principle was simple: automation beats willpower every time. Not discipline. Not tracking. Not motivation. Systems that run without you when you can't.

That same system that kept our finances running during 22 seizures and endless therapy appointments has now helped 2,175 families save over $5.3 million combined in the last year alone. These families had real challenges   and limited time. They succeeded because they had a system that worked in real life.

Traditional financial advice assumes your biggest challenge is motivation. That if you just tried harder, tracked more, wanted it enough, you'd succeed. But you already work hard. You're already motivated. What you're missing isn't willpower - it's a system designed for how high earners actually live.

The Six-Figure Freedom Formula recognizes three truths about your life that other systems ignore:

First, you have maybe 30 minutes monthly for money management. Not 30 minutes daily. Not weekly budget meetings. Monthly.

Second, you can't put life on hold while you "focus on finances." Kids need rides. Work demands attention. Parents need help. The system has to run while life happens.

Third, you've worked too hard to live like you're broke. You need to build wealth while keeping the life you've built.

The Six-Figure Freedom Formula works as a complete operating system for your money that runs automatically while you live your life.

Let me show you exactly how it works.

The Three-Step Framework

The Six-Figure Freedom Formula breaks down into three phases that work together from day one:

Track Your Money: Know exactly where you stand without daily tracking.

Grow Your Money: Build wealth automatically while paying off debt.

Protect Your Money: Bulletproof your progress against life's curveballs.

Other systems make you choose: pay debt or save, invest or build emergency funds, focus on today or plan for tomorrow. This approach doesn't match how high earners' lives work. At your income level, parallel progress isn't just possible - it's essential.

Think about how you handle complex projects at work. You often don't complete phase one entirely before starting phase two. You run multiple tasks at once, each supporting the others. Your money should work the same way.

Inside Budget Dog Academy, families at your income level typically uncover thousands in recoverable money their first month - not through restriction, but through fixing what's broken.

Let me share what some Budget Dog Academy members discovered when they applied these principles.

One member found nearly $850 a month disappearing into forgotten subscriptions. Another saved about $630 a month by paying off a car loan and lowering insurance costs. A third discovered his 401(k) fees were quietly costing him thousands every year.

None of them changed their lifestyle. They just built better systems.

Why Corporate Frameworks Beat Consumer Budgets

You already know how to manage complex projects at work. You create systems. You set up processes that run without your constant attention. You review progress monthly, not minute by minute.

The Six-Figure Freedom Formula applies that same systematic thinking to your money:

- **Automatic payments and savings**: Everything runs without daily effort
- **Smart alerts**: You only hear about problems that need attention
- **Monthly reviews**: One check-in to keep everything on track
- **Clear priorities**: Your money follows rules you set once

Most budgeting apps assume you want to spend hours categorizing purchases. The Formula assumes you want to spend 30 minutes monthly making sure everything's running smoothly.

This is why high earners succeed with this system when they've failed with others. You're not learning something new. You're using skills you already have.

Here's the surprise: the most successful Academy members don't have finance degrees. They're managers, engineers and consultants. They already know how to run systems at work. They just never applied it to money.

The Multiplication Effect

When all three steps work together, something remarkable happens. Your progress accelerates beyond what any single approach could achieve.

What catches people off guard is that the Formula actually requires LESS effort than fixing one thing at a time. When everything runs together, you set it up once and it keeps working. When you do things one by one, you're constantly starting and stopping.

Debt falls faster because you're not depleting savings for emergencies. Investments grow steadily because automation removes emotion. Protection increases because you're building multiple safety nets at the same time.

Each part makes the others stronger. That's why Academy families see such big changes in their first year. They don't use extreme methods. They use smart planning.

This same system that helped us eliminate $304,000 in debt proved its worth during Logan's medical crisis. Because we'd already used it to become debt-free, we could focus entirely on her care while our automated systems kept everything running perfectly.

In the next section, I'll show you exactly how Step 1 stops the bleeding without changing how you live.

Step 1 - Stop the Bleeding (Without Changing Your Life)

Step 1 of the Six-Figure Freedom Formula finds money you're already losing without knowing it.

This is the Track Your Money phase. You won't track every expense like budget apps want. Instead, you'll see the complete picture of where your money actually goes.

Most high earners discover they're bleeding more than $2,000 every month through invisible leaks. Forgotten subscriptions. Services you pay for twice. Investment fees nobody explained. Insurance overlap. Interest you don't need to pay.

One Academy member realized she was spending almost $3,000 more each month than she thought — mostly on subscriptions and services she didn't need. Another cut costly advisor fees after learning how to manage her investments on her own.

Another realized she was paying for the same gym in a few different ways — monthly fees, extra charges, and services she no longer used.

These people weren't careless with money. The leaks were invisible until the system revealed them.

The Track Your Money phase uses three simple reports that work together. These show you the truth about your money. Not to shame you. Not to restrict you. Just to show where money really goes.

These reports take less than an hour to set up. Then they update by themselves. No daily tracking. No receipt scanning. Just clarity about where you stand.

The money you need is already in your income. It's just getting lost. Step 1 finds it without changing how you live.

But finding the leaks is just the beginning. Step 2 shows you something counterintuitive - how to build wealth faster by NOT focusing all your money on debt.

Step 2: Build Real Wealth (While Keeping Your Lifestyle)

Step 2 does something most financial advice says you can't do: build wealth while you keep your lifestyle and pay off debt.

This is the Grow Your Money phase. Instead of confusion about "which account first," you'll follow a clear order that captures free money first, then builds tax-free wealth, then uses every other opportunity.

The Formula shows you exactly where each dollar should go and why. You'll stop leaving employer matching on the table and missing years of growth. You'll build wealth NOW, not someday. While your debt falls, your investments grow. While bills get paid, retirement accounts build. Everything happens at the same time.

One member found out he was missing thousands in employer matching while focusing only on paying down debt. That's like refusing free money to pay a 5% loan. The Formula fixed his priorities right away.

The Grow Your Money phase automates these contributions. Your money flows to the right places without you thinking about it.

Step 3: Bulletproof Your Future (Against Any Crisis)

Step 3 protects everything you've built. This is the Protect Your Money phase. It's what kept our finances intact during Logan's medical crisis.

Many people think protection means insurance. That's only part of it. True protection means your wealth keeps building even when life hits hard.

The Protect Your Money phase creates multiple safety layers. Not just an emergency fund in savings. A complete system that handles anything life throws at you.

First comes crisis-proof automation. Your bills and investments continue even if you can't manage them for months. When we lived in the hospital with Logan, nothing fell through the cracks. Not through discipline - through systems that ran without me.

Next comes emergency reserves sized for your life.

Not the generic "3 - 6 months expenses" everyone suggests. The Formula calculates what YOU need based on your job, your family's health, and your bills. Some families need three months. Others need nine.

The Formula shows your number.

Then there's wealth protection. Making sure your money isn't being drained by hidden costs. This means checking insurance coverage, investment fees, and taxes regularly.

One family found they had too much life insurance but not enough disability coverage - a gap that could have ruined them.

Finally, marriage protection. Money stress breaks up marriages. The Formula includes systems that keep both partners informed without constant money talks. Automatic reports you both see. Clear rules you agree on once. No more fights about spending.

Even if your partner doesn't care about budgets or spreadsheets, they'll appreciate the simplicity.

Members often say their partners now join the money talks — because the system makes it simple enough for everyone to follow.

The Protect Your Money phase isn't about fear. It's about building systems so strong you never worry. Your wealth grows automatically. Your family stays protected. Your marriage stays strong.

When Logan's crisis hit, this system meant I could focus on her care. Not on money. Not on bills. Just on what mattered - getting her well.

Why Everything Happens at Once (Not One at a Time)

The real power of the Six-Figure Freedom Formula comes from running all three steps together. When Track, Grow, and Protect work as one system, your results multiply instead of just adding up.

Traditional advice tells you to focus on one goal at a time. Pay off all debt first, then save, then invest. This sounds logical but ignores how high earners' lives actually work.

You can't pause emergencies while paying debt. You can't skip years of investment growth while building savings. At your income level, doing one thing at a time is actually slower than doing everything together.

When Academy families implement all three steps together, they see surprising results. Not because they're doing anything extreme, but because the system creates benefits that build on each other. Each step strengthens the next.

Consider what happens when you only focus on debt elimination. Every unexpected expense becomes a setback that adds months to your timeline. Your car needs repairs, so you skip debt payments or worse, add to credit cards.

Without protection systems, you're always vulnerable to life's surprises.

But when you run all three steps together, that same car repair comes from your emergency fund. Debt payments continue automatically. What would have been a three-month setback becomes a minor adjustment.

The multiplication effect shows up clearly in the numbers. Families who use the complete Formula often see progress much faster than those focused only on debt — because it helps them stay on track and avoid common setbacks.

They're not paying more toward debt or working harder. They're just using a system that prevents the setbacks that derail most people.

This matters more now than ever. Technology is replacing jobs faster than ever before. The safety net you build today protects you from becoming obsolete tomorrow. Running all three steps together means you have backup plans for your backup plans - exactly what you need when job security doesn't exist anymore.

One Academy member described how this changed everything for her family. Before the Formula, they would make progress for a few months, then an emergency would erase their gains.

After setting up all three steps, those same emergencies became manageable. Their debt continued falling, investments kept growing, and protection funds handled surprises without derailing progress.

Another member paid off $40,000 in credit card debt while simultaneously building emergency reserves - something that would have been impossible focusing on just one goal.

Beyond the numbers, something else changed for these families. The Sunday night anxiety disappeared. The tension in their marriages eased. They stopped lying awake at night wondering which bill to skip. Money became boring - in the best possible way.

This step-by-step approach saved our family during Logan's medical crisis. While managing daily hospital life and medical bills, our automated systems kept every financial obligation on track.

Bills got paid automatically. Investments grew. Our protection systems handled the enormous unexpected costs. Even during our hardest year, our net worth improved.

At your income level, you have the cash flow to build wealth, eliminate debt, and protect your family simultaneously. The Formula simply shows you how to make these goals work together so they reinforce each other instead of competing for resources.

Why Dave and Ramit Won't Work for You

You've probably tried other financial systems. Maybe you bought Dave Ramsey's books or downloaded Ramit Sethi's courses. You might have even made some progress before things fell apart.

These popular systems don't work for high earners because they weren't designed for your situation.

Dave Ramsey's Baby Steps were designed for people drowning in debt with limited income. His system assumes you have time for daily budget meetings and cash envelopes. It assumes you'll live on "rice and beans" while attacking debt with the intensity of a gazelle.

That works if you're making $40,000 with credit card debt. But at your income level, the math changes completely.

Cutting your grocery budget from $1,500 to $500 monthly saves $1,000. But finding and eliminating the $2,000 in hidden leaks you don't even know about? That's more effective and doesn't require your family to sacrifice their quality of life.

Ramsey's approach also ignores opportunity cost. While you're throwing every penny at debt, you're missing employer 401(k) matches and years of compound growth. For someone making $40,000, that might be worth it. For someone making $150,000, you're literally throwing away wealth to follow rules designed for a different situation.

Ramit Sethi takes the opposite approach. He assumes you've already handled the basics and just need to optimize. His advice focuses on automation and psychology, which helps, but skips the foundational systems high earners desperately need.

His approach assumes your debt is already manageable. That you just need to negotiate better rates and invest more aggressively. But what if you're carrying $300,000 in student loans? What if you have the income but can't figure out where it goes?

Most high earners fall somewhere between these two extremes. You're not broke enough for Dave's emergency approach. You're not organized enough for Ramit's strategies.

You need something designed specifically for your situation. High income, high complexity, high demands on your time.

The Six-Figure Freedom Formula works because it's built from the ground up for people exactly like you - people who can't spend hours on money management but need professional-grade systems that run automatically.

The truth is, you don't need another guru. You need a system that fits your actual life.

The Difference Between Knowing and Doing

The Six-Figure Freedom Formula isn't theory. It's a proven system that's already working for 2,175 families who were exactly where you are now.

They had the same doubts you're probably feeling. Can a system really be this simple? Will it work with my specific situation? What if I'm too far behind to catch up?

One member started with negative net worth and increased it by $640,516 in just 20 months. Another saw $106,000 net worth gain in six months. These aren't outliers - they're people who followed the Six Figure Freedom Formula.

Here's what they discovered: the Formula works regardless of your starting point. Whether you're dealing with $50,000 in debt or $500,000. Whether you're 30 or 50. Whether you have one child or five.

The system adapts to your situation while maintaining the core framework that makes it effective.

This book gives you everything you need to implement the Formula. The three-step framework. The automation strategies. The exact order for building wealth. You have the complete system.

Some people excel with just the book. They take these concepts, apply them in the right order, and transform their finances independently.

Others benefit from additional support - whether that's through Budget Dog Academy, finding an accountability partner, or working with a financial advisor who understands high earner challenges.

The difference between those who transform their finances and those who stay stuck isn't intelligence or income. It's taking action with the right system.

You have three choices from here.

You could do nothing. Keep managing everything in your head while money leaks through invisible gaps. That's another $12,000 to $18,000 gone to invisible leaks. Another $6,000 in missed employer matching. Another year of compound growth lost forever. A year from now, you'll be $25,000 poorer than you needed to be.

Worse, you'll still have that Sunday night dread. You'll still be fighting about money. You'll still be wondering why you make good money but never get ahead. The stress compounds just like the lost interest you're not earning.

You could try piecing together your own system from conflicting advice. Some people make this work, but most get overwhelmed and give up within months.

Or you could implement the Formula you've just learned. Start with Step 1 tomorrow. Set up the Track Your Money phase. Begin the automation that changes everything.

The framework is clear. The path is proven. Your financial transformation starts with the first step.

In Chapter 5, I'll walk you through the exact three financial statements that make the Track Your Money phase work.

The first statement alone typically uncovers more than $2,000 a month that high earners never knew they were losing.

The second shows you where your money actually goes versus where you think it goes.

But it's the third statement that changes everything - because it reveals the one number that predicts whether you'll build wealth or stay stuck, and no budget app or financial advisor will ever show it to you.

Enjoying the book? We'd love to hear from you.

If you're open to sharing which strategies or insights have resonated with you, we'd love to send you a free gift as a thank you. Scan the QR code to record a quick video testimonial and get **free access to Budget Dog's Ultimate Investing Bundle**—covering index funds, investing 101, 401(k)s, crypto basics, and debt payoff strategies.

Visit the QR code above or go to
review.sixfigurefreedombook.com
to share your thoughts and claim
your free course bundle.

CHAPTER 5:

THE 3 STATEMENTS THAT WILL CHANGE EVERYTHING

I promised to show you the three financial statements that make the Track Your Money phase work.

At the moment you might be checking multiple accounts, trying to piece together your financial picture. Maybe you avoid looking altogether because it's overwhelming. Or maybe you have a system that sort of works but still leaves you uncertain about where you really stand.

These three statements change that. They're the same framework Fortune 500 companies use to track billions, simplified for family finances.

The first one is your Budget – which is really an Income and Expense statement as it shows exactly where every dollar goes each month. When you see it laid out, you'll spot the leaks immediately.

The second is your Balance Sheet. This tracks what you own versus what you owe. Most people have never calculated their actual net worth. When you do, you might be surprised - sometimes in a good way, sometimes not.

The third is your Amortization Schedule. That's just a fancy way of saying "your debt payoff timeline." This one shows exactly when each debt disappears if you keep paying what you're paying now.

Together, these three statements reveal everything about your money.

Inside Budget Dog Academy, we teach families to build these statements in their first month. They typically find over $2,000 in monthly leaks they never knew existed. Money that was simply disappearing.

One of our members, found she could trim expenses and redirect $2,731 monthly toward her goals. The statements showed her exactly where the overspending was happening.

You don't need special software. You don't need to be good at math. You just need to see the truth about where you stand.

But first, forget everything you think you know about budgeting. This isn't about tracking every penny or feeling guilty about coffee. This is about finding money you're already spending unconsciously and redirecting it toward what actually matters.

Statement 1: Budget - Where Your Money Actually Goes (vs. Where You Think)

Most people think budgeting means tracking every penny and feeling guilty about spending. That misses the point.

Your Budget statement is just a spending plan. It shows what comes in, what goes out, and what's left over. That's it.

Here's how Budget Dog Academy teaches it: Start by looking back at your last three months of bank statements. Create two columns: Income and Expenses.

In the Income column, add up everything that came in - your paycheck, side income, tax refunds, everything. Get the monthly average.

In the Expenses column, list what actually went out.

Group similar things together - all restaurants under "Dining Out," all subscriptions under "Subscriptions," all insurance payments under "Insurance."

Don't overthink the categories. Just group things in a way that makes sense to you. Add it all up and get your monthly average.

This becomes your starting point - what you actually spent, not what you think you spent.

When you do this, you'll see patterns you never noticed. Let me show you how this works.

Imagine Sarah, a project manager earning $165,000, who thought she was breaking even each month. When she looked back at three months of actual spending, she found:

- Income: $8,500 monthly
- Necessary expenses: $6,300
- Unaccounted for: $2,200

Her checking account never had $2,200 extra, so where was it going? When she dug deeper, she found:

- Random Target runs she couldn't remember: $400
- Subscription services she forgot she had: $250
- Restaurant meals beyond her planned dining budget: $500
- Amazon purchases that "didn't count": $350
- Cash withdrawals she couldn't track: $300
- Miscellaneous charges under $20 that added up: $400

This wasn't money sitting in her account. It was money bleeding out through what Budget Dog Academy calls "unconscious spending" - purchases that happen without thought, bring little value, and are forgotten within days.

Often, people who insist they have "no money left" are right - the money is gone. But when they see where it actually goes, they're shocked. Not at how much they spend on the necessities, but at how much disappears into things they can't even remember buying.

Once you see where money actually goes, you can take control. Plan next month before it starts. Assign every dollar. In this example, Sarah ended up redirecting her $2,200 toward student loans.

Those extra payments mean the loans will be paid off three years earlier. Three years of freedom found in one hour of looking at bank statements.

Here's exactly how Sarah might restructure her next month:

- Income: $8,500
- Rent: $2,500
- Groceries: $800
- Insurance: $400
- Car payment: $450
- Utilities: $350
- Gas: $300
- Planned dining budget: $200
- Other necessities: $1,300
- **Redirected to student loans**: $2,200

Before this exercise, that $2,200 was leaking out unconsciously. Now it has purpose. Every dollar knows where to go before the month starts.

The setup takes about an hour. After that, ten minutes monthly keeps you on track. The anxiety disappears immediately.

Set this up once, automate your bill payments and savings transfers, then just check monthly to ensure everything's running. You know exactly what you can spend. No checking bank balances. No guilt. Just clarity.

When families we work with do this exercise, they find what Sarah's example shows - money bleeding out unconsciously (inside the Academy we use automated systems that track this without the manual work).

But this simple approach gives you the same clarity. The same control. The same freedom from money anxiety.

One more thing: this works best when you simplify your financial life. One checking account. One savings account. One main credit card. Every extra account is another potential leak. Academy families often close 3-4 unnecessary accounts in their first month.

The thing is, finding that money is only half the equation. The next statement reveals whether you're actually building wealth or slowly going broke.

Statement 2: Balance Sheet - The Truth About What You're Really Worth

Right now, you're probably making financial decisions blind.

Should you pay off debt or invest? Should you buy that rental property? Take the job with an equity bonus? You're guessing because you don't know where you actually stand.

Your net worth is the only number that tells you if you're winning or losing financially. Your salary doesn't tell you. Your home value doesn't tell you. Only your net worth will show you if you're building wealth or slowly going broke.

Without knowing this number, you could be making six figures while sliding backwards. You could be sitting on more wealth than you realize. You have no idea which one you are. Your Balance Sheet calculates this number.

Every month you don't know this number, you make decisions that could be destroying wealth. Consider Tom, who lost three years of compound growth before he figured this out.

So write down the value of everything you own. Subtract everything you owe. That's your net worth. One number that changes every financial decision you make.

Here's what this might look like. Consider Tom, who makes $140,000 a year:

What He Owns (Assets):

- House value: $385,000
- 401k: $87,000
- Savings: $8,000
- Car value: $22,000
- Total Owned: $502,000

What He Owes (Liabilities):

- Mortgage: $298,000
- Student loans: $85,000
- Car loan: $15,000
- Credit cards: $12,000
- Total Owed: $410,000

Net Worth: $92,000

In his situation, he avoided doing this for years, afraid of what he'd find. When he finally did it, that $92,000 shocked him. He wasn't broke. He'd been building wealth without realizing it.

The psychological shift was immediate. The vague anxiety about money disappeared. He had a real number to work with.

Every financial choice became clear. Pay off the credit cards first - highest interest, biggest impact on net worth. Skip the new car - it would drop his number. Max out the 401k match - guaranteed growth.

That number became his scoreboard - he went from avoiding his finances to actually wanting to check them.

Some people discover negative net worth. They owe more than they own. That's common for high earners with big mortgages and student loans. But knowing beats guessing. You can't improve what you don't measure.

Update this every three months - March 31, June 30, September 30, and December 31. Save each version. Watch the trend. In Tom's case, his net worth grew $18,000 his first year just from making better decisions once he could see the impact.

Budget Dog Academy families who track this number report significant net worth growth in their first year - often tens of thousands to hundreds of thousands of dollars. Not from earning more. From redirecting money once they see the whole picture. The impact on your mental state alone makes this worth doing.

The calculation takes 30 minutes. The clarity lasts forever. Once you build this, updating it takes 5 minutes quarterly. Set a calendar reminder for the last day of each quarter. Done.

But there's a third statement that changes everything. It's the one that shows you exactly when you'll be free. Not 'someday', but an actual date.

Statement 3: Amortization Schedule - Your Debt-Free Date (Down to the Day)

Most people talk about debt in vague terms. "Someday I'll be debt-free." "Eventually the student loans will be gone." "We'll pay off the house before retirement."

This vagueness keeps you trapped. Without a specific date, debt feels permanent. You make minimum payments hoping things will somehow work out. Years pass. The balances barely move.

Your Amortization Schedule, or debt payoff timeline changes that. It shows exactly when each debt disappears if you keep paying what you're paying now. No wishful thinking. Just math.

Here's how this might look. Consider Michael, who builds his amortization schedule:

Current Debts:

- Credit Card #1 ($8,000 at 24% interest, $250/mth): Paid off May 2027
- Credit Card #2 ($5,000 at 22% interest, $150/mth): Paid off Sept 2027
- Car Loan ($22,000 at 5% interest, $450/mth): Paid off March 2029
- Student Loans ($45,000 at 7% interest, $550/mth): Paid off June 2033

Wonder if your debt load is reasonable for your income?
Our Debt to Income Ratio Calculator at
sixfigurefreedombook.com/resources
shows whether you're overleveraged
compared to other high earners.

Suddenly "someday" became June 15, 2033. That's when his last payment would post. That's when he would be free.

The psychological impact can be immediate. Seeing that 2033 date - realizing his kids would be in middle school before his student loans were paid off - created urgency to take action.

But here's where the timeline becomes powerful. You can change the dates.

In this example, Michael had found $1,800 in unconscious spending from his Budget statement. He ran the numbers again, putting that $1,800 toward debt using the avalanche method (highest interest first):

New timeline with $1,800 Extra:

- Credit Card #1: Paid off September 2025 (saved 20 months)
- Credit Card #2: Paid off December 2025 (saved 21 months)
- Car Loan: Paid off August 2026 (saved 31 months)
- Student Loans: Paid off March 2028 (saved 63 months)

He bought back over 5 years of his life with money he was already spending on nothing.

Building this timeline takes 30 minutes. List each debt. Note the balance, interest rate, and minimum payment. Use any free online calculator to find the payoff date. Then play with the numbers.

What if you add $100 extra? $500? Or the money you found in your Budget statement?

> **To see exactly how extra payments change your freedom date, use our Debt Paydown Calculator at sixfigurefreedombook.com/resources.**
> It shows month-by-month how additional payments compound to save you years.

Budget Dog Academy families eliminate debt 28 months faster on average once they see these dates. Not through extreme sacrifice. Through clarity about what each extra dollar buys them - time.

Inside the Academy we use sophisticated tracking systems that update these timelines automatically. But a simple list and a calculator work just as well.

The power isn't in the tool. It's in seeing that debt has an end date, and you control when that is. Build this once. Update only when you add or eliminate a debt. The timeline runs itself.

Why One Without The Others Keeps You Stuck

Here's what most people miss: these three statements aren't separate tools. They're one complete system that shows you everything.

Watch how they work together in Michael's case:

His Budget statement revealed $1,800 in unconscious spending, similar to Sarah's example. His Balance Sheet showed negative $50,000 net worth (owing more than he owned). His Amortization Schedule showed freedom in 2036.

Now he could make smart decisions with complete information.

That $1,800 could go toward debt, eliminating it by 2031 instead of 2036. Or split it - $900 to debt, $900 to investments, becoming debt-free in 2033 while building wealth. Or build emergency savings first, protecting against setbacks that would make everything worse.

Without all three statements, you're guessing. With them, the path becomes obvious.

The Balance Sheet shows whether you should prioritize debt or investing. If you have negative net worth, debt reduction usually wins. If you're positive but heavily leveraged, you might split focus.

The Budget statement finds the money to execute your plan. No need for rice and beans. Just redirect unconscious spending toward conscious goals.

The Amortization Schedule shows the impact of every decision. Add $200 to debt payments? See exactly how many months earlier you're free. Choose investing instead? Know exactly what you're trading.

Here's how someone might use all three statements together. Jennifer, a marketing director, uses these to transform her finances in one year:

- Found $1,500 monthly in unconscious spending
- Discovered her net worth was $35,000
  (better than expected)
- Saw debt freedom was 8 years away with
  minimum payments

She split the $1,500: $1,000 to debt, $500 to investing. Result: Debt freedom moved up 3 years. Net worth jumped to $62,000. All without changing her lifestyle.

When you can see all three statements together, every financial decision becomes obvious in a way it never was before.

Budget Dog Academy families use these three statements as their foundation. Some track them manually with templates. Others use automated systems.

Both approaches work. The magic isn't in how you track them - it's in seeing all three pieces of your financial puzzle at once. And when you do, every financial decision becomes obvious.

You'll know exactly whether to pay off debt or invest. You'll see which expenses are actually keeping you poor. You'll understand why some people making half your income are building wealth faster.

Build These Before Monday

You can build these three statements this weekend. Here's exactly what to do:

Friday evening (1 hour):

- Pull your last 3 months of bank statements.
- Look at what you actually spent.
- Build your Budget statement.
- Find your unconscious spending.

Saturday morning (30 minutes):

- List everything you own and owe.
- Create your Balance Sheet statement.
- Calculate your net worth.
- Face the real number, whether it's better or worse than expected.

Saturday afternoon (30 minutes):

- List all debts with balances, interest rates, and minimum payments.
- Use any free online calculator to find payoff dates.
- Build your Amortization statement (debt-payoff timeline).
- See exactly when you'll be free.

By Sunday, you'll have complete financial clarity for the first time.

FREE TOOLS TO BUILD YOUR STATEMENTS:

- Money Leaks Calculator - Find your hidden spending
- Debt Paydown Calculator - See your freedom date
- Debt to Income Ratio Calculator - Check if you're overleveraged
- Cost of Inaction Calculator - See what waiting costs you

All available at
sixfigurefreedombook.com/resources

The $2,000 Monthly Wake-Up Call

Most people find three surprises when they complete these statements:

First, they're bleeding more than $2,000 a month through unconscious spending. Money that could build wealth is evaporating on things they can't remember buying.

Second, their net worth isn't what they imagined. Sometimes they're worth more than they thought (retirement accounts add up). Sometimes less (debt accumulated faster than realized). Either way, knowing beats guessing.

Third, they can be debt-free years earlier than they thought. Not through extreme sacrifice. Just by redirecting money that's already being spent on nothing valuable.

Curious what waiting another month costs you?
Our Cost of Inaction Calculator at
sixfigurefreedombook.com/resources
shows the real price of delay.

Take Jennifer's example again - she found $2,500 monthly she didn't realize was leaking. Her net worth was positive $35,000 despite feeling broke. She could be debt-free three years earlier just by being intentional with money she was already spending.

The statements reveal the truth. No judgment. No shame. Just clarity about where you stand and what's possible.

Some people prefer working through this with guidance and community support. Inside Budget Dog Academy, we provide both - plus automated systems that eliminate the manual work. We work with a limited number of families each year, focusing our energy on ensuring each family actually transforms their finances rather than just learning about it.

But many succeed with just these templates and their own determination. The system works either way. The difference is in the journey, not the destination.

The Truth About Your Financial Blind Spots

These three statements will show you something no financial advisor or budget app ever will: the complete, unfiltered truth about your money.

You'll see where it's really going (not where you think it goes). You'll know what you're actually worth (not what you hope or fear). You'll discover when you'll be free from debt (not "someday" but an actual date).

This truth might be uncomfortable at first. In Sarah's example, she discovered she was spending $2,200 monthly on nothing. In Tom's example, he realized he'd been feeling broke with $92,000 in net worth. In Michael's example, the debt timeline showed it wouldn't be gone until his kids were in college.

I remember my own moment of truth - seeing I'd need to work until 67 just to break even. The number made me physically sick. But that nausea turned into determination.

But truth is where transformation begins. You can't fix what you won't face.

The 2,175 families who've saved over $5.3 million using these exact statements all started the same way - by building these three documents and facing their financial truth.

In Chapter 6, I'll show you what to do with that money you're about to find. There's a specific order for investing that most high earners get completely backwards, leaving hundreds of thousands of dollars on the table. The investment account hierarchy I'll share with you actually multiplies your wealth while you sleep - but only if you follow the exact sequence.

But first, build these three statements this weekend. Before another month of unconscious spending disappears. Before another year passes wondering why you can't get ahead despite earning good money.

These three statements - available as bonus templates at sixfigurefreedombook.com/resources - give you all you need to transform your finances.

The 2,175 families inside Budget Dog Academy use automated versions that pull data directly from their accounts, but the core system you're learning here is identical. The only difference is they save 20 minutes monthly on data entry.

Your financial transformation starts this weekend. Build these three statements. See your complete financial truth. Then use that clarity to make decisions that actually build wealth.

In Chapter 6, I'll show you exactly what to do with the money you're about to find. There's a specific investment sequence that multiplies wealth - and most high earners get it completely backwards.

CHAPTER 6:

WHY MOST HIGH EARNERS SHOULD INVEST BACKWARDS

Here's what happens when you start making good money. You open investment accounts and start putting money away for retirement. You feel responsible and smart about your future.

But there's a specific order that makes your money work harder. Most people get this order completely backwards.

Most high earners start with regular investment accounts - called "taxable" accounts because you pay taxes on any money your investments make. These feel sophisticated because they're unlimited and flexible. You can invest in anything, anytime.

Meanwhile, they leave money sitting in basic employer accounts that seem boring or limited. They skip special tax-advantaged accounts because the contribution limits feel small compared to their income.

This backwards approach costs them thousands yearly in unnecessary taxes and missed opportunities.

The Six-Figure Freedom Formula flips this order. It captures every tax advantage and guaranteed return first, then uses flexible accounts last.

But most high earners never learn the correct sequence, costing themselves hundreds of thousands over their careers.

Why Your 'Sophisticated' Investment Strategy Is Actually Costing You

High earners fall into what I call the sophistication trap. You assume that because you're successful professionally, you need complex investment strategies to match your income level.

This shows up in predictable ways. You research individual stocks because picking winners feels more skilled than buying boring index funds. You open multiple investment accounts across different companies because diversification sounds smart. You avoid your company's 401k because the investment options seem limited compared to what you can buy elsewhere.

Charles Schwab studied this pattern in 2024. They surveyed 1,200 affluent households and found that 49% admitted to "chasing advanced strategies" before they had maximized their basic tax-advantaged savings. This cost them an average of $19,000 annually in lost tax efficiency.[1]

Complexity feels smart, but it costs money.

Take investment fees as an example. When you buy individual stocks or actively managed funds, you often pay higher fees than simple index funds. These fees seem small - maybe 1% or 2% annually. But on a $100,000 account, that's $1,000 to $2,000 yearly in extra costs.

Over 20 years, those extra fees can cost you $50,000 to $100,000 in lost growth. You pay tens of thousands extra for the privilege of likely getting worse returns than a basic index fund.

The same thing happens with account selection. You might open accounts with three different investment companies because you want access to specific funds or features. But managing multiple accounts creates more work for you and often means you miss opportunities to consolidate and simplify.

Meanwhile, you're still not maxing out the free money and tax breaks available through simpler accounts.

One Academy member, a software engineer, fell into this exact pattern. He had accounts with four different investment companies, buying individual tech stocks because he felt he had an inside edge. When we calculated his results, he was losing over $30,000 annually by investing in the wrong order - missing employer matches while paying unnecessary fees and taxes.

After using the Six-Figure Freedom Formula order, he automated his entire investment plan and could have hundreds of thousands more at retirement.

I see this pattern everywhere - brilliant professionals making expensive mistakes because complex feels smarter than simple.

The Six-Figure Freedom Formula works differently. It prioritizes guaranteed returns before uncertain ones. It uses tax advantages before paying unnecessary taxes. It automates the boring stuff so you can focus on what actually matters in your life.

The Account Sequence That Multiplies Your Money While You Sleep

Most people think all investment accounts work the same way. You put money in, hopefully it grows, and you take it out later. But different types of accounts have completely different tax rules that can save or cost you thousands yearly.

The Six-Figure Freedom Formula uses a specific order that gets every tax break and free dollar available to you. Here's the exact sequence:

First: Get your employer match

Your employer offers free money through your 401k or 403b. Don't turn it down.

Here's how it works: If your company matches 6% of your salary, you put in 6%. They double your money. If they match up to $3,000, you put in $3,000. They give you another $3,000.

Set this up through your paycheck. The money comes out before you see it. You won't miss what you never had.

Second: Buy company stock at a discount (if available)

Some companies let workers buy their stock for less than it costs everyone else. This is called an ESPP.

If your company offers 15% off, that's like buying a $100 bill for $85. You can often sell it right away and keep the $15 profit.

Sign up when your company has open enrollment. The money comes from your paycheck over six months.

Third: Open your own IRA

An IRA is your personal retirement account. It's separate from your job. You control it.

You can save $7,000 each year. If you're 50 or older, you can save $8,000.

If you aim to move $583 from your bank each month, that adds up to around $7,000 for the year.

Pick between two types:

- **Traditional IRA:** Pay less taxes now, pay taxes later when you retire
- **Roth IRA:** Pay taxes now, never pay taxes on this money again

Fourth: Put more in your 401k

After you do the first three steps, add more to your 401k.

Here's how much you can put in total for 2025:

- Under 50 years old: $23,500
- 50 to 59 years old: $31,000 (you get an extra $7,500)
- 60 to 63 years old: $34,750 (you get an extra $11,250 if your company offers it)
- 64 or older: Back to $31,000

The higher limit for ages 60-63 is new. Not all companies offer it yet. Ask your HR department.

Try to save 15% of your income between all accounts. Many companies will increase your savings by 1% each year until you hit your goal.

Fifth: Health Savings Account

If you have a high-deductible health plan, you can open an HSA. This is the best tax deal out there.

You can save:

- **Single person:** $4,300 per year
- **Family:** $8,550 per year
- **55 or older:** Add another $1,000

Why HSAs are amazing:

- **No taxes** when you put money in
- **No taxes** while it grows
- **No taxes** when you use it for medical bills

Set up monthly transfers from your bank. For a single person, that's about $358 per month.

Next Step: Taxable investment accounts

After you've worked through the priority above - employer match, ESPP (if offered), IRA, continue 401(k) to about 15% of income, and HSA if you qualify - put any extra into a regular taxable account.

These regular accounts don't get tax breaks. You pay taxes on any money you make. But they're still good because you can use the money anytime you want.

Set up automatic monthly transfers here too. Just like the other accounts.

The Bottom Line

Follow these steps in order. Each one builds on the last. Start with the free money from your employer. End with regular investment accounts.

If you make good money, this system can save you $15,000 to $25,000 every year in taxes. Plus you get all the free money from your employer.

This isn't complicated. Set things up once. Then everything runs on autopilot while you build wealth.

The Free Money You're Leaving On The Table

Your employer match isn't just free money - it's the best investment return you'll ever get, guaranteed.

Here's how employer matching actually works. Let's say you make $100,000 and your company matches up to 6% of your salary. If you contribute $6,000 to your 401k, your employer adds another $6,000. You just earned a 100% return instantly, before any market growth happens.

Even if your investments lose money that year, you're still ahead because your employer doubled your contribution.

But most people don't take full advantage. Vanguard's data shows the average person only contributes enough to get about half their available match.[2] They're leaving thousands yearly on the table.

Why does this happen? Usually because people don't understand the math, or they think they can't afford to contribute more from their paycheck.

At a 24% bracket, a $6,000 pre-tax contribution effectively costs about $4,560 after taxes. Your employer adds $6,000 - an instant return well over 100% on your net cost.

Compare that to any other investment. The stock market averages about 10% yearly over long periods. Your employer match gives you 100% to 194% on day one.

Employee Stock Purchase Plans work similarly when your company offers them. These plans let you buy company stock at a discount, usually 10% to 15% off the market price.

Some plans are even better. They might let you buy stock at a 15% discount from either the price at the beginning or end of a six-month period - whichever is lower. This can create instant gains of 20% to 30% or more.

One Academy member ignored her company's stock purchase plan for years because she thought it was too complicated. When she finally signed up, she was able to buy company stock at a 15% discount every six months - essentially getting free money she'd been leaving on the table.

Even when she sold the stock immediately to avoid concentration risk, she pocketed $750 every six months. That's $1,500 yearly for filling out a form once.

The math on employer benefits is unlike anything else in investing. These aren't market predictions or investment theories. They're guaranteed returns written into your employment contract.

Yet many employees miss part of their employer match when they don't contribute at least the plan's match threshold—typically around 6% of pay.

The Six-Figure Freedom Formula always captures these guaranteed returns first. Everything else comes after you've collected every dollar your employer is willing to give you.

Every month you delay getting your full employer match costs you years of compound growth you'll never get back.

The HSA Secret Weapon High Earners Ignore

Remember step five in the investment sequence - the Health Savings Account? Most people gloss right over this one, but it's actually the most powerful tax advantage available to investors.

There's one account that gives you better tax benefits than any other investment option available. It's called a Health Savings Account, or HSA.

To use one, you need to have a high-deductible health insurance plan. Many people avoid these plans because the deductible seems scary - you might have to pay $3,000 to $7,000 out of pocket before insurance kicks in.

HSAs are special because they give you triple tax advantages.

First, you don't pay taxes on the money you put in. Just like a traditional 401k, your HSA contributions reduce your taxable income for the year.

Second, your money grows tax-free while it sits in the account. No taxes on investment gains, dividends, or interest.

Third, you don't pay taxes when you take the money out - as long as you use it for medical expenses (before age 65, using it for non-medical expenses triggers taxes plus a 20% penalty).

No other account gives you all three benefits. Even Roth IRAs only give you two of the three.

For 2025, you can contribute $4,300 if you're single or $8,550 for a family.[3] If you're over 55, you can add another $1,000.

Often people miss this: you don't have to spend HSA money right away. You can let it grow for decades and use it in retirement when medical costs are typically higher.

After age 65, you can even use HSA money for non-medical expenses without any penalty. You'll pay regular income tax on those withdrawals, just like a traditional IRA. But all the medical expenses you have after 65 - and there will be many - come out tax-free.

The average couple retiring today will spend about $300,000 on medical costs during retirement.[4] With an HSA, all of that could be tax-free money.

One Academy member started maximizing his HSA in his mid-thirties. He contributes the full family amount annually and invests it in index funds, just like his other retirement accounts. He pays his current medical expenses out of pocket and keeps all the receipts.

By retirement, this strategy could grow his HSA to significant six figures - all available tax-free for qualified medical expenses.

Want to see exactly how your retirement contributions will grow?
Use the Academy's Compound Interest Calculator at
sixfigurefreedombook.com/resources
to project your HSA, 401k, and IRA balances at retirement. Most high earners are amazed by the tax-free
wealth they can build.

Meanwhile, he can still reimburse himself for those medical expenses he paid out of pocket decades earlier. There's no time limit on HSA reimbursements as long as you keep your receipts. The expense must be incurred after your HSA is opened, and you need to keep clear records.

When you pay yourself back later, that withdrawal is tax-free - and once withdrawn, you can use that money however you want.

But most high earners miss this opportunity. IRS data shows only 9% of eligible households contribute the maximum to their HSAs.[3] They focus on maxing out 401ks and IRAs while ignoring the account with the best tax benefits.

The catch is that HSAs aren't available to everyone. You do need a high-deductible health plan, and your employer has to offer HSA compatibility.

If you qualify, make it a priority after your match, IRA, and continuing your 401(k) until you're saving about 15% of income - then fund taxable accounts.

Think of your HSA as a stealth retirement account that happens to cover medical expenses along the way. But there's one strategy that can save you even more than the triple tax advantage - and it's completely legal.

The 'Backdoor Roth' Revelation

Most high earners don't realize you can still contribute to a Roth IRA even if you make too much money to qualify normally. Without the backdoor Roth, high earners leave $200,000+ in tax-free growth on the table over their careers.

First, let me explain why you'd want a Roth IRA. With a regular investment account, you pay taxes on any money your investments make. With a traditional 401k or IRA, you get a tax break now but pay taxes later when you withdraw the money in retirement.

A Roth IRA works differently. You pay taxes on the money you contribute now, but then everything - your contributions and all the growth - comes out completely tax-free in retirement. No taxes on decades of compound growth.

The problem is the IRS sets income limits for Roth IRA contributions. For 2025, if you're single and make more than $165,000, or married and make more than $246,000, you're locked out of Roth IRAs completely.[5]

But there is a legal work-around called the "backdoor Roth conversion."[6]

Instead of contributing directly to a Roth IRA, you contribute to a traditional IRA first. There are no income limits for traditional IRA contributions - anyone can put money in.

Then, immediately after you make the contribution, you convert that traditional IRA money to a Roth IRA. **Watch the pro-rata rule:** if you hold other pre-tax IRA balances, part of the conversion becomes taxable. Many people roll old IRAs into a 401(k) first to avoid this.

You'll pay taxes on the conversion, but since you just put the money in, there's usually little or no growth to tax.

The result is the same as if you had contributed directly to a Roth IRA. You paid taxes on the money going in, and now it will grow tax-free forever.

You can do this every year with the full $7,000 contribution limit (or $8,000 if you're over 50). That's $7,000 annually that will never be taxed again, no matter how much it grows.

Consider how the backdoor Roth strategy works over time. Contributing $7,000 annually for 15 years means $105,000 in contributions.

If investments grow at typical market rates, that could grow to around $340,000 - all tax-free with a Roth.

Compare that to a traditional IRA, where you'd owe regular income tax on all withdrawals. In a 25% tax bracket, that could mean roughly $85,000 in taxes on that $340,000 - the backdoor Roth could save tens of thousands over time.

Most CPAs know about this strategy, but many don't mention it unless you ask specifically. Some investment companies make the process complicated with extra paperwork and waiting periods.

But once you understand the steps, it becomes routine. You make the traditional IRA contribution in January, convert it to Roth in February, then repeat the process next year.

The backdoor Roth fits perfectly into the investment sequence we covered earlier. After you max out your employer match and before you move to taxable accounts, use this strategy to get tax-free growth on $7,000 annually.

For high earners who feel locked out of Roth benefits, this opens the door to decades of tax-free compound growth.

Why You Should Max Out 'Boring' Accounts Before 'Exciting' Ones

This is where most high earners get the investment order completely backwards.

You probably feel drawn to taxable investment accounts because they seem more advanced. No contribution limits. Complete flexibility. Access to any stock, bond, or fund you want. The ability to trade whenever you feel like it.

Meanwhile, accounts like 401ks and IRAs feel restrictive. Limited investment options. Annual contribution caps. Penalties if you withdraw money early. They seem basic compared to the unlimited possibilities of a regular brokerage account.

Those 'boring' restricted accounts will make you significantly more money over time.

You can either prioritize tax-advantaged accounts first, then add taxable accounts, or split contributions from the start. We recommend prioritizing tax-advantaged first.

If you're earning $150,000, you're probably in the 24% marginal tax bracket.[7] Every dollar you put in a traditional 401k or IRA saves you $0.24 immediately in taxes. That's a guaranteed return before your investments even start growing.

So that $20,000 contribution only costs you $15,200 out of your actual paycheck. You're investing with Uncle Sam's money as well (the $4,800 portion you would have otherwise paid in tax), not just your own.

In a taxable account, that same $20,000 comes entirely from your after-tax income. Plus, you'll pay taxes on any dividends, interest, or gains while the investments grow. Then you'll pay taxes again when you sell.

Over 20 years, this difference adds up to six figures of extra wealth in the tax-advantaged accounts.

Don't get me wrong, the pull of taxable accounts is strong. You can check your balance anytime. You can sell whenever you want. You feel like you're in complete control.

Tax-advantaged accounts on the other hand, require patience. You're basically agreeing to lock up your money until retirement in exchange for massive tax benefits. For many high earners, this feels like giving up control.

The truth is, you should think of taxable accounts as your last choice for investing, not your first choice. After you've followed the priority and captured the key tax advantages, then move to taxable accounts.

Most high earners have the income to max out all their tax-advantaged space. In 2025, that's:

- $23,500 in your 401k (or $31,000 if you're 50-59, or $34,750 if you're 60-63)*
- $7,000 in an IRA (or $8,000 if you're 50 or older)
- $8,550 in an HSA for families (or $9,550 if you're 55 or older)
  Check to see if your company offers the new higher limit

That's $39,050 annually in contributions that get better tax benefits.

Once you've worked through the priority above - your employer match, ESPP (if offered), IRA, continuing your 401(k) until you're saving about 15% of income, and your HSA (if you qualify) - then consider taxable accounts.

Following this order can still save you $15,000 to $25,000 a year in taxes while building the same wealth.

The Six-Figure Freedom Formula puts guaranteed tax savings before the feeling of flexibility. Boring accounts that work beat exciting accounts that cost you money.

But there's one decision that paralyzes most high earners - should you pay off debt or invest?

After all, you've found the money in Chapter 5, you know the investment sequence, but you also have student loans, a mortgage, and maybe some credit card debt.

Do you put your extra money toward debt or follow the investment hierarchy? Do you pay off the house early or max out retirement accounts? What about that car loan - should you eliminate it first or let it ride while you invest?

This decision has trapped more high earners in financial paralysis than any other choice. I've watched brilliant professionals research this for months while losing $2,000+ each month to indecision.

The framework that I show you in Chapter 7 will end this debate forever and challenge everything you think you know about debt.

And what's more surprising, is that most financial advisors get this completely wrong.

CHAPTER 7:

THE 'WHATEVER LETS YOU SLEEP AT NIGHT' SOLUTION

Here's something no financial expert will admit: there is no perfect answer to the debt versus investment question.

Dave Ramsey says pay off all your debt first. Period. No exceptions.

Investment advisors say you're losing money if you pay off a 4% mortgage when you could be earning 10% in the market.

Meanwhile, you're stuck in the middle, researching endlessly while losing money every single day you don't decide.

"I second-guess every decision and end up doing nothing," one Academy member told me recently. She'd been paralyzed for over a year, unable to choose between paying debt or starting her retirement investments.

Another member spent over a year researching the 'perfect' debt payoff method. Should he pay the smallest debts first for quick wins? Or the highest interest rates for mathematical efficiency? While he researched, his credit card balances continued to grow by thousands.

Northwestern Mutual studied this exact problem in 2023. Financial procrastination costs high earners an average of $16,850 annually.[1] That's money lost just through indecision.

That's $1,400 every month. Gone. Just from indecision. In ten years, that's $168,000 lost. That could pay for college. Or let you retire early. Gone because you couldn't decide.

You know what's worse? The decision you're agonizing over probably matters less than you think. The difference between a good strategy and a perfect one is tiny compared to the difference between doing something and doing nothing.

The Six-Figure Freedom Formula takes a completely different approach to this decision. One that respects both your intelligence and your emotions.

Let me show you the framework that finally ends this debate forever. But first, you need to understand why every piece of advice you've heard so far has been designed to fail someone in your exact situation.

The Six-Figure Freedom Formula Philosophy

Budget Dog Academy teaches something different from every other system out there. We teach: "My rule is to do whatever lets you sleep at night."

This is about recognizing that the best financial plan is the one you'll *actually* follow.

Think about your last diet. You probably researched the perfect meal plan. Calculated exact calories. Bought special foods. How long did it last? Two weeks? A month?

Money works the same way. A perfect plan you quit beats a good plan you maintain for decades.

The Certified Financial Planner Board studied this in 2023. People who picked comfortable approaches stuck with them 29% longer than people who picked "optimal" but stressful plans.[2]

Over time, the comfortable approach built more wealth. Not because it was mathematically better, but because it was actually followed.

When you're earning six figures, the math difference between strategies shrinks anyway. Whether you pay off a 5% loan or invest at 8% returns matters less than whether you consistently put $2,000 monthly toward either goal.

A reader wrote to us to say: "I was paralyzed for months trying to choose between debt payoff and investing. Once I accepted that either choice was fine as long as I picked one, I finally started making progress."

That's the permission I'm giving you right now. Stop searching for the perfect answer. Pick the approach that lets you sleep at night and stick with it.

The Hybrid Decision Framework

Inside Budget Dog Academy, we use a simple framework that helps you decide where your extra money should go. We call it the hybrid decision because most people don't choose all-or-nothing approaches.

Here are your four options:

1. **Save it all** - Build your emergency fund first
2. **Attack debt only** - Focus everything on becoming debt-free
3. **Invest it all** - Start building wealth while paying minimums on debt
4. **Split it up** - Put some toward each goal simultaneously

There's no universally correct choice. But there is a correct choice for you, based on your situation and psychology.

If you have zero emergency savings and that terrifies you, option one makes sense. Nothing else matters if a car repair sends you into more debt.

If your debt feels like a weight on your chest every morning, option two brings relief. Some people need to see those balances dropping monthly to stay motivated.

If you're comfortable with debt and worried about missing years of compound growth, option three works. This usually fits people with low-interest debt like mortgages.

But here's what's interesting - Fidelity found that 44% of high-income households choose option four.[3] They split their extra cash between debt and investing. Over five years, these families built 21% more net worth than families who chose just one focus.

Why? Because the hybrid approach works for both the part of you that wants the best returns and the part that wants to feel secure. You're making progress on everything. No regrets. No second-guessing. But there's a hidden complexity for high earners that makes this choice harder than it should be.

The Decision-Making Difficulty That High-Earners Face

When you're earning $150,000 or more, this decision gets harder than most advice admits.

You're not dealing with just one debt. You've got several. Student loans at 6% interest. Car loan at 4%. Mortgage at 3%. Maybe credit cards at 22%. Each one needs its own decision.

On top of that, you've got investment opportunities pulling at you. Your employer matches your retirement contributions.

That's an instant 100% return. You could open tax-free accounts. You could invest in the stock market.

The UBS Global Wealth Report found that 67% of households earning over $150,000 juggle three or more types of debt.[4] These same families also have to decide about retirement matches, tax-saving accounts, and investment options.

Simple advice like "pay off all debt first" doesn't work when you're losing free money from your employer by following it.

Here's what you're really trying to figure out:

- Should you skip the employer match to pay debt faster?
- Does paying off a 3% mortgage make sense when prices go up 4% a year?

You're also wondering about the tax break on mortgage interest. And whether to max out your 401(k) or pay off student loans.

A client captured it perfectly: "Which accounts first - 401(k) with match, IRA, or brokerage? I need someone to just show me the order."

The confusion makes sense. Every financial expert has different advice. Some care most about making the highest returns. Others want you to reduce risk. Many forget about taxes completely.

You need a plan that looks at everything but stays simple enough to actually do. Let me show you the framework that took me $304,000 in debt to figure out.

The Framework That Finally Ends The Debate

Instead of giving you more tools to confuse you, let me show you the exact framework that helped us decide what to do with our $304,000 in debt.

The framework is simple: run the numbers on both extremes, then find what feels right in between.

Here's how it works. Say you have an extra $1,000 each month after paying minimums on everything. You've got $50,000 in debt at 5% interest. Without extra payments, it'll take you ten years to pay it off.

First, figure out what happens if you throw all $1,000 at the debt.

Using any online calculator, you'll find that $1,000 extra means you're debt-free in three years instead of ten. That saves you seven years of payments and thousands in interest.

But for those three years, nothing goes to investments. Zero compound growth during that time. After year three, you can invest the full $1,534 (your old debt payment plus the extra $1,000). By year ten, your investment account would have about $173,000.

Second, figure out what happens if you invest all $1,000 instead.

You keep paying minimums on the debt for the full ten years. But you're investing $1,000 monthly the entire time. At typical market returns of 8%, your investment account would grow to about $183,000 after ten years.

Want to run these exact numbers for your situation?
Use our Debt Paydown Calculator at
sixfigurefreedombook.com/resources.
It shows you three scenarios side-by-side so you can see exactly how different approaches change your timeline.

Now here's where it gets interesting - and where most people never look.

What if you split it? Put $500 toward debt and $500 toward investing?

The debt takes about four and a half years to disappear. Not as fast as three years, but much better than ten. Meanwhile, you've been investing $500 monthly. After the debt's gone, you add that debt payment to your investing. By year ten, your investment account would have about $177,000.

Look at your three options:

- **All debt:** Free in 3 years, investment account worth $173,000 by year ten
- **All investing:** Debt for 10 years, investment account worth $183,000 by year ten
- **Split approach:** Free in 4.5 years, investment account worth $177,000 by year ten

The difference between the best and worst? About $10,000 over ten years. That's $1,000 per year. Less than $100 per month.

But the psychological difference? Massive.

With the all-debt approach, you get freedom fast but miss three years of market growth. With all-investing, you carry debt stress for a decade. With the split, you get steady progress on both.

A member put it perfectly: "Once I saw the numbers were all pretty close, I picked what felt right. I went 70% debt, 30% investing. The debt disappeared faster than pure math would suggest because seeing progress motivated me to find extra money."

This is what I mean by 'do whatever lets you sleep at night.' The math difference is smaller than you think. The psychological difference decides if you'll stick with it.

Why Your Anxiety Beats The Math Every Time

A mathematically perfect choice, while completely logical, could be the worst financial choice that you can make. Let me explain.

Math says invest if you can earn 8% while your debt costs 5%. You come out ahead by 3%. Simple.

But math doesn't wake up at 3 AM worried about losing your job. Math doesn't feel sick when you see an $80,000 student loan balance. Math doesn't have a spouse who gets anxious every time a credit card statement arrives.

I knew a wealthy advisor who chose the 'wrong' strategy on purpose. He told me: "I'd rather sleep well than squeeze out another percent."

The American Psychological Association studied this. People who pick strategies that feel comfortable stick with them 18% longer.[5] They reach their goals more often than people who pick "perfect" but stressful plans. The math isn't wrong, but we all need to sleep at night.

I learned this when my daughter Logan was diagnosed with Dravet syndrome. We had already paid off our debt before her diagnosis, which turned out to be one of the best decisions we ever made.

When you're living in a hospital, watching monitors, managing seizures, the last thing you need is financial stress on top of medical stress. Having no debt meant one less burden during the worst time of our lives.

Your emotions aren't weakness. They're information about what you'll actually stick with.

One Academy member earning in the high six figures chose pure debt payoff even though the math favored investing. She couldn't focus at work with substantial debt hanging over her.

Once she committed to debt elimination, her performance improved and she earned a significant raise. The peace of mind created more value than investment returns would have.

Another member went the opposite way. His mortgage rate was under 3% while inflation was running higher. Paying it off early felt like losing money to him, so he invested any extra income he had. The debt didn't bother him - missing market growth did.

Both made the right choice because both picked strategies they could follow for years.

The strategy that keeps you awake will fail. The strategy that lets you sleep will succeed. Even if the math disagrees.

How To Start Without Drowning In The Details

The hardest part isn't making the decision to get started - it's getting started and resisting the urge to overcomplicate it all.

You don't need seventeen spreadsheets. You don't need to perfect every penny. You just need to pick your approach and set it up once.

Here's exactly how to start any of the three approaches:

If you're going all-in on debt: Set up one extra automatic payment to your highest-rate debt. That's it. When that debt dies, move the payment to the next one. Don't overthink the order - highest rate first saves the most money.

If you're going all-in on investing: Open one investment account if you don't have one. Set up one automatic monthly transfer. Buy one broad market index fund. The whole setup takes an hour.

If you're splitting between both: Cut your extra money in half. Set up two automatic transfers - one to debt, one to investing. Adjust the split after a few months if needed, but start with 50/50.

One high earner spent six months building the 'perfect' tracking system while nothing got paid off or invested.

Meanwhile, someone earning less set up two automatic transfers in 20 minutes and made real progress. The lesson: the simple system that runs beats the complex system that never starts.

The fancy system that never starts loses to the simple system that runs every month.

Research shows that people who automate their finances are far more likely to reach their goals than those who try to manage payments manually.

You can perfect it later. You can't get back the months you waste planning instead of doing.

Your Freedom Date, Down To The Month

Once you make the debt versus investment decision, the Six-Figure Freedom Formula shows you exactly what that choice means for your future - it shows you specific dates and dollar amounts.

If you choose debt payoff, you'll see the exact month each debt disappears. March 2026 for the credit cards. October 2028 for the student loans. June 2031 for the mortgage. You can circle these dates on your calendar.

If you choose investing, you'll see exactly how much your account will hold at specific ages. $50,000 by age 40. $250,000 by age 50. $1 million by age 58. Real numbers you can plan around.

If you choose the hybrid approach, you'll watch both numbers change each month. Debt drops by $1,200 while investments grow by $800. Progress you can track.

Vanguard studied this in 2024. People with specific targets and dates built 24% more wealth over five years than people with vague goals.[6] When you know the exact destination, it changes how you travel.

One member explained how seeing specific dates changed her decision-making. When the calculator showed that extra monthly payments would mean debt freedom years earlier - coinciding with her son's high school graduation - the choice became obvious.

Another member went the opposite direction. When they saw that consistent monthly investing would build significant wealth by their mid-fifties, they stopped feeling guilty about keeping their low-rate mortgage. They could see the trade-off clearly.

Both made confident choices because they could see exactly where each path led.

Set It Once And Forget It Forever

Once you've decided where your money goes, automation makes it happen without you.

Set up your chosen approach once. Review it monthly for 30 seconds to make sure it's running. That's your entire commitment.

No more lying in bed wondering if you remembered to make the extra payment. No more guilt about missing a month because life got busy. No more decision fatigue from choosing what to do with extra money every paycheck.

The system runs while you live your life.

Vanguard found that automatic systems work. When people set up automatic increases, their savings grow without them having to think about it.[7]

Automation means your money works while you sleep. While you're dealing with work deadlines, family emergencies, or just living your life, your debt shrinks and your investments grow.

One member who automated a split approach eliminated significant debt while simultaneously building an investment portfolio. The system ran automatically without requiring constant attention or decisions.

That's what happens when you choose once and let the system run.

Enough Planning. Time To Build Wealth

You've spent enough time researching. You know the framework. You've seen the numbers. Now it's time to choose.

The Six-Figure Freedom Formula doesn't require the perfect choice. It requires a choice you'll stick with. Whether that's attacking debt with everything you've got, investing while paying minimums, or splitting the difference - pick what lets you sleep at night.

Set it up this week. Make it automatic. Then get on with your life while your money works in the background.

In Chapter 8, I'll show you how to run your entire financial system - debt, investing, bills, and savings - in just 30 minutes monthly.

No more hours of spreadsheet management. No more financial panic on Sunday nights. Just a simple monthly routine that keeps everything on track while you focus on what actually matters to you.

But first, make your debt versus investment decision. This week. Because another month of analysis paralysis costs you real money.

Your future self will thank you for choosing progress over perfection.

Enjoying the book? We'd love to hear from you.

If you're open to sharing which strategies or insights have resonated with you, we'd love to send you a free gift as a thank you. Scan the QR code to record a quick video testimonial and get **free access to Budget Dog's Ultimate Investing Bundle**—covering index funds, investing 101, 401(k)s, crypto basics, and debt payoff strategies.

Visit the QR code above or go to
review.sixfigurefreedombook.com
to share your thoughts and claim
your free course bundle.

CHAPTER 8:

YOUR 30-MINUTE MONEY MACHINE

You're about to simplify your entire financial life down to 30 minutes a month.

No more checking three banking apps before breakfast. No more Sunday night spreadsheet marathons. No more lying awake wondering if you remembered to pay the credit card.

Let me show you exactly how.

One Account, One Card, One System.

Most people think they need multiple accounts to be financially sophisticated. Separate savings for vacation and emergencies. Different credit cards for different rewards.

Budget Dog Academy teaches the opposite: you only need one checking account, one savings account, and one credit card.

This probably feels wrong. What about maximizing rewards? What about different savings goals?

The challenge is that multiple accounts create mental work you can't afford.

Picture your typical Sunday night.

You need to check if you have enough money for the week. With seven accounts, that means seven logins. Seven passwords to remember (or reset because you forgot). Seven balances to add up in your head. Seven places where an automatic payment might have failed.

By the time you figure out where you actually stand, you've burned 45 minutes and your stress levels are through the roof.

Now imagine one checking account. One quick look tells you everything. Your balance is clear. Your available funds are obvious. No mental math needed.

The time savings alone make this worth doing. When one Academy member went from eleven accounts to three, his monthly money check went from four hours to 30 minutes. That's three and a half hours back every month.

But the real benefit is mental clarity. When money is scattered everywhere, you never really know where you stand. You might have $2,000 in one account, $500 in another, $1,200 somewhere else. But can you spend $300 on groceries? Who knows - it depends which card you use and which account it pulls from.

This confusion leads to mistakes. Overdraft fees when you have money sitting in another account. Missed payments because you forgot about that one credit card. Late fees on accounts you don't check regularly.

With one system, these problems disappear. One checking account for all income and bills. One savings account for your emergency fund. One credit card for all purchases (paid off monthly from that one checking account).

The setup is simple. Pick the checking account where your paycheck already goes. Open one high-yield savings account online - they pay 4-5% interest instead of the 0.01% your regular bank offers. Choose one credit card with simple cash back rewards.

Then close everything else. Transfer any balances to your main accounts. Update any automatic payments. Delete those extra banking apps from your phone.

This feels wrong at first. Like you're losing something important. But within a month, you'll wonder why you ever juggled so many accounts. The mental relief is immediate. The time savings compound every month.

But there's a specific way to set this up that most people get completely wrong - and it determines whether your system survives a crisis.

Your Monthly Money Meeting (Yes, Just Monthly)

You already have the three statements from Chapter 5. But there's a specific timing sequence that makes them take just 30 minutes instead of 3 hours.

Budget Dog Academy families follow a simple review schedule that takes 30 minutes monthly, five minutes quarterly, and an hour annually.

Here's an example monthly routine:

Third Sunday of every month, 8 PM:

- Open your three statements (Budget, Balance Sheet, Amortization Schedule)
- Check that all automatic payments went through
- Verify investment contributions happened
- Adjust next month's spending plan based on what's coming up

Done.

That's the entire monthly review. No daily expense tracking. No weekly budget meetings. Once a month for 30 minutes.

The timing matters. Third Sunday gives you a full week before month-end to adjust anything. Evening works because markets are closed and you can see final balances. Pick a time when the kids are in bed and you won't be interrupted.

Charles Schwab's 2024 research backs this up. Couples who schedule regular financial check-ins report fewer money conflicts and are more likely to stick to their spending plans.[1]

The quarterly review (March 31, June 30, September 30, December 31) takes five minutes. Update your Balance Sheet with current account values. See if your net worth is growing. That's it.

The annual review happens every January. Spend an hour checking insurance coverage, updating investment allocations, and setting the next year's goals. Most people do this while watching football on New Year's Day.

This schedule works because it matches the rhythm of how money actually moves. Bills are monthly. Net worth changes quarterly. Tax and insurance decisions are annual.

Put these reviews in your calendar right now. Monthly money meeting - third Sunday, 8 PM. Quarterly net worth update - last day of each quarter. Annual review - New Year's Day. Set them to repeat forever.

When the reminder pops up, you'll spend 30 minutes instead of avoiding it for hours. Doing it regularly removes the dread. It becomes as routine as your Monday morning team meeting at work.

The automation I'm about to show you is what makes this 30-minute system possible. Without it, you're back to hours of manual work.

Set This Up Once, Never Touch It Again

Once you've simplified to one checking account, one savings, and one credit card, automation becomes powerful. But there's a specific order that makes everything work without you thinking about it.

Most people automate randomly. They set up their mortgage payment, maybe their phone bill, then forget about the rest. This creates a mess where some bills are automatic, others aren't, and you're never sure what's actually happening.

The Six-Figure Freedom Formula automates in layers, with the most important stuff happening first.

Layer 1: Income arrives (Day 1-2 of the month) Your paycheck hits your checking account. If you're paid twice monthly, the system still works - just run it twice.

Layer 2: Move protection money (Day 3) Emergency fund savings transfers automatically to your high-yield savings. This happens before you see the money or pay any bills. Most people set this at $500-1,000 monthly until they hit their target.

Layer 3: Investment contributions (Day 4) Your Roth IRA contribution leaves your checking account. Your extra 401k contribution comes from payroll. HSA money transfers if you have one. This money is gone before you can spend it.

Most people set up this part of their automation backwards - bills first, investments last. That's why they never build wealth.

Layer 4: Fixed bills (Day 5-10) Mortgage or rent comes first. Then car payment, insurance, student loans, utilities. Every bill that stays the same each month gets pulled automatically between day 5 and 10.

Layer 5: Credit card payment (Day 20) Your entire credit card balance gets paid from your checking account. Not the minimum - the whole thing. This forces you to only spend what you actually have.

Layer 6: What's left is yours (Day 21-31) What's left in your checking account is available for entertainment, dining out, and daily life. When it's gone, you're done spending for the month.

Savings and investments happen first (before you can talk yourself out of them). Bills get paid before you accidentally spend that money. And you know exactly what's left over to spend on the fun stuff.

One of our Academy members set this up in one afternoon. She used to juggle payment dates in her head constantly. Now she knows that by the 20th, everything important is handled - the mental relief is immediate.

Vanguard's 2025 research shows that automatic features drive record participation rates - people who automate their savings and investments are far more likely to stay on track long-term.[2] They succeed through systems that run automatically.

The setup takes two hours total. Log into each account. Set up the automatic transfers. Pick the dates. Then stop thinking about it.

Every payment happens without your involvement. Every savings goal gets funded without willpower. Every investment gets made without you deciding each month.

The system runs while you sleep, work, vacation, or deal with life's emergencies. That's the entire point - it works when you can't. Which is exactly what I discovered during the worst four months of my life.

What Happens When Life Falls Apart

The real test of any financial system isn't how it works when everything's perfect. It's what happens during crisis.

I discovered this in the worst possible way. Logan's first seizure happened during a normal Tuesday. Within hours, we were learning medical terms no parent wants to know. Within days, our life had shifted from conference rooms to hospital rooms.

For four months, the hospital became our home. I learned which vending machines had the least-stale sandwiches. Which waiting room chairs were almost comfortable enough to sleep in. How to read monitors that tracked things more important than any spreadsheet.

During those four months, I never once logged into our bank. Four months of zero financial management.

Yet everything kept working. Our utilities stayed on. Investment contributions happened on the fifteenth. Insurance premiums got paid automatically. Our financial life continued on autopilot while we focused on keeping our daughter alive.

This wasn't luck. It was the automation we'd set up months before, running exactly as designed.

But automation alone wouldn't have been enough. We needed layers of protection that planned for the worst:

Here's what saved us during Logan's crisis:

First protection layer: Everything on autopilot - Bills and investments all happened automatically. I didn't have to remember anything or make any transfers. The system ran itself.

Second layer: Emergency fund in place - We had six months of expenses sitting in our high-yield savings. When medical bills started hitting, we could pay them without touching our regular system.

Third layer: My wife had full access - Both our names were on every account. She knew all the passwords. She could run everything if I couldn't. During one three-week stretch when I never left the hospital, she handled what little needed handling.

Fourth layer: Simple enough to explain - When my mother-in-law offered to help, I could explain our entire system in five minutes. One checking account. One credit card. Everything automatic. She could check that things were working without needing a finance degree.

This isn't about planning for some vague future emergency. Life could hit you hard at some point. Job loss. Medical crisis. Family emergency. Divorce. The system needs to work when you can't.

Set up your automation assuming you won't be there to run it. Because someday, you may not be.

From Chaos to Clockwork

You now have the complete 30-minute monthly system. One checking account. One savings. One credit card. Everything automated in the right order. Protection layers for when crisis hits.

Without this system, the average high earner loses 60 hours annually to financial management - that's a full work week and a half. Plus the mental cost of constant money stress.

The setup takes one weekend. List your accounts. Close the extras. Set up the automatic transfers in the order I showed you. Put the monthly review in your calendar.

No more research needed. No more perfect system to find. This one is tried and tested.

Every month you delay costs you real money. The mental energy spent juggling accounts. The fees hiding in accounts you rarely check. The missed opportunities while you search for something better.

When families group it all together, they often discover forgotten fees and subscriptions that have been draining their accounts for months or years.

Simplifying this alone saves most families two hours monthly. That's 24 hours yearly you get back. The automation saves another three hours monthly from not having to manually move money and pay bills. Together, you're getting five hours of your life back every month.

More importantly, you're getting peace of mind. No more Sunday night panic about whether bills got paid. No more checking multiple accounts to see if you can afford something. No more wondering if you forgot something important.

In Chapter 9, I'll show you what most people never think about until it's too late - how to protect everything you've built when life truly falls apart. Because having money isn't enough if a crisis can wipe it all out.

But first, set up your automation this week. Before another month passes with money scattered everywhere and no system running it.

Your 30-minute monthly money machine starts now.

CHAPTER 9:

WHEN LIFE HITS HARD (AND IT USUALLY WILL)

People often say "life happens."

We know this in our heads, but emotionally I've found we often dismiss it (as if that will keep accidents, illnesses, crises, and death away from us).

Pretending bad things won't happen doesn't protect you. It just guarantees you'll be unprepared when they do.

I've seen what happens to families who go through this exact situation. High earners who thought their income would protect them, until it stopped coming.

Right now, you might think your six-figure income is your safety net. That the next promotion will finally give you security. That your 401(k) balance means you're protected.

But when you're facing massive medical bills and you can't work for six months, suddenly that $180,000 salary means nothing. The income stops but the bills don't.

According to Kaiser Family Foundation research, families facing severe medical crises lose a median of $161,000 in total wealth.[1]

I've worked with families who went through this. Lost income while dealing with the emergency. Emergency borrowing at terrible rates because they needed cash immediately. Draining retirement accounts early and eating the penalties.

The prepared families? They maintained their lifestyle through the entire crisis. Their disability insurance replaced their income. Their emergency fund handled the immediate costs. Their proper health coverage meant manageable bills, not bankruptcy.

The unprepared families lost everything. Same income, same crisis, but protection determined who survived financially.

This system kept us afloat through our worst nightmare.

My five-month-old daughter Logan had 22 seizures in one year. We made 18 ER visits.

The medical bills topped $200,000 by month eight. Yet our automated systems kept our finances running smoothly during that same nightmare year while we lived in and out of hospitals.

The difference wasn't luck. It was preparation.

The Day My Five-Month-Old Saved Our Financial Future

January 29, 2022. My daughter Logan was five months old. I was preparing for a company presentation when my wife Erin came running in, hysterical, saying something was terribly wrong with our baby.

Logan was having her first seizure.

The presentation I'd spent three days preparing still glowed on my screen. The quarterly numbers that seemed so important five seconds ago meant nothing now.

That day started a journey that would include 22 seizures in 2022 alone. Eighteen ER visits. Eleven extended hospital stays. Two trips to Texas for specialized care. By the eighth month, medical bills had topped $200,000.

Our daughter, who appeared perfectly healthy, was diagnosed with Dravet Syndrome. It's a rare condition that affects one in every 15,700 children.[2] It ranges from mild seizures to severe developmental challenges, and in 15-20% of cases, death.

I'd recently left Deloitte and we had just become debt-free months earlier after paying off our house and any remaining debt. Thankfully, we'd kept all our protection systems in place even after the debt was gone.

Not because I predicted Logan's diagnosis - nobody could have. But because I'd learned that life throws curveballs when you least expect them.

During those endless nights watching monitors, I realized something: Being debt-free mattered more than I'd imagined. What mattered was that income kept flowing, immediate costs were covered, and medical bills wouldn't destroy what we'd built.

The protection we'd kept in place - even after becoming debt-free - gave us the ability to focus entirely on Logan instead of money.

Meanwhile, in that same hospital, I met families earning similar incomes who had no protection. One couple had to sell their house to pay for treatment. Another dad went back to work two weeks after his son's diagnosis because without disability coverage, no work meant no income.

That could have been us. Same income level. Same crisis. Completely different outcome.

The difference wasn't that we were debt-free or wealthy. It was that we'd protected ourselves before we thought we needed it.

Logan's crisis taught me that protection isn't optional for high earners. It's the foundation everything else depends on. Yet most of us protect everything except what matters most.

Why Your Income Is Your Biggest Unprotected Asset

You insure your car worth $30,000. You insure your house worth $400,000. But most high earners never insure their ability to earn $180,000 a year.

Think about that math.

If you're 35 and earn $180,000 yearly until 65, that's 30 years of income. Thirty years times $180,000 equals $5.4 million.

UBS research shows only 42% of affluent households carry disability insurance that replaces at least 60% of their income.[3]

Your ability to earn is worth more than everything else combined. Your house, your retirement accounts, everything. But you leave it completely unprotected.

Inside Budget Dog Academy, we see this pattern constantly. Families protect everything except what actually pays for everything. They'll research car insurance for hours to save $20 monthly. But they won't spend ten minutes getting disability coverage.

The math can get scary here. Social Security disability pays about $1,400 monthly.[4] That's it. Try covering your $3,000 mortgage on $1,400. Against a $3,000 mortgage and $11,000 in monthly expenses, that $1,400 is meaningless. Try buying groceries. Paying car payments. It doesn't work.

One Academy member discovered this gap during Week 12 of the program—earning nearly $200,000 but with every type of insurance except disability. He figured his savings would cover him.

When we ran the numbers together, his family's monthly expenses meant his emergency fund would only last six months.

After that? He'd have to drain his retirement accounts and pay huge penalties. Probably sell the house. Maybe move in with relatives.

He got disability insurance that week for a few hundred dollars monthly, which would replace 60% of his income if he couldn't work.

Months later when he was injured and couldn't work for an extended period, that insurance saved his family from losing everything.

The worst part? He almost didn't buy it. He spent three weeks debating whether $180 monthly was "worth it."

That's $180 to protect $5.4 million in future income. You spend more on streaming services and gym memberships. Yet those won't save your family when you can't work.

The Three Layers Of Protection Every Family Needs (But Only 7% Have)

Most families have random pieces of protection. Some life insurance from work. Maybe decent health coverage. Possibly an outdated will from when they bought their house.

But protection doesn't work in pieces. It needs layers that work together when crisis hits.

Budget Dog Academy teaches three essential layers:

Layer One: Income Protection - This goes beyond basic disability insurance. You need term life insurance if something happens to you, disability insurance if you can't work, and an emergency fund for immediate needs. Each piece backs up the others.

Layer Two: Asset Protection - Your protection should roughly match your net worth. Umbrella insurance covers you beyond your auto and home policies - usually $1–2 million in extra protection for about $200 a year. Add proper health insurance with a reasonable out-of-pocket maximum so medical bills don't destroy you even with coverage.

Layer Three: Legacy Protection - If you can't make decisions, who does? Without proper documents, the state decides.

You need an updated will that says who gets what, healthcare power of attorney so someone can make medical decisions if you can't, and financial power of attorney so bills get paid if you're incapacitated. Plus beneficiaries updated on every account so money transfers without probate.

Most people grab pieces randomly. They get life insurance when their first kid is born. Add disability when someone at work gets cancer. Write a will when they buy a house.

But these pieces don't talk to each other. Your life insurance might pay out while your family has no idea how to access it because you never set up financial power of attorney. Your disability might kick in but your spouse can't pay bills because their name isn't on the accounts.

Build these layers in order: income protection, then assets, then legacy documents. Each layer assumes the others exist and work together.

Households that had core protections in place - an emergency fund, proper insurance, and basic estate documents - reported stronger financial resilience and lower stress during emergencies.

But there's one mistake I see high earners make over and over that destroys their protection before they even need it.

The "I'm Young and Healthy" Trap That Costs Millions

The biggest protection mistake high earners make? Waiting until they think they need it.

"I'll get life insurance when we have kids." "I'll buy disability coverage when I'm older." "I'll update my will when there's actually money to leave."

This thinking costs families millions.

But here's what makes waiting even more dangerous.

The real killer isn't the price, it's that you might not qualify at all.

Inside Budget Dog Academy, we had a member learn this the hard way – a healthy 33-year-old consultant earning $220,000.

One member kept putting off disability insurance because he felt invincible. Then during a routine physical, they found slightly elevated blood pressure. Nothing serious - his doctor wasn't even concerned. But that single reading meant he either couldn't get disability coverage at all or faced significantly higher premiums.

The cost of waiting tripled his monthly premium - turning what would have been affordable into thousands extra annually for decades.

The even scarier part? Once you have any health issue, every insurance company can see it. They share a database called MIB that tracks every application and medical issue.[5] One kidney stone, one anxiety prescription, one abnormal blood test - suddenly you're either declined or paying fortune for coverage.

It's best to get maximum coverage while you're young and healthy, then reduce it later if needed. You can always decrease coverage. You can't always get it in the first place.

The sweet spot is your early thirties. You're earning enough to afford proper coverage but still young enough for the lowest rates. Lock in your insurability before life decides you're uninsurable.

The Term Life Secret That Saves High Earners $500,000

Insurance salespeople will avoid telling you this simple fact: term life insurance beats whole life insurance for 99% of high earners.

Let me prove it with actual numbers.

What I'm about to show you is the exact math that made three different insurance agents hang up on me during office hours. Once you see these numbers, you'll understand why agents push certain products so desperately.

Here's how the comparison breaks down.

Whole life insurance sounds sophisticated because it lasts your entire life and builds cash value. The salesperson shows you charts of money growing inside your policy, using phrases like "be your own bank" and "tax-free retirement income."

What they don't tell you is the massive price difference between term and whole life. A 35-year-old pays about $50 monthly for

$1 million in term life coverage, but that same million in whole life costs $750 monthly or more.

The salesperson says term insurance is "just renting" while whole life is "owning." But let's do the math they're hoping you won't do.

Take that $700 monthly difference. Instead of giving it to the insurance company, invest it in a basic index fund. After 30 years at 8% returns, you'd have about $940,000.

The whole life policy after 30 years? Maybe $400,000 in cash value. And here's the catch - that $400,000 isn't extra money. It's part of your million dollar death benefit. When you die, your family gets the million, not the million plus the cash value.

Inside Budget Dog Academy, we teach a simple rule: buy term and invest the difference. Get a 20 or 30-year term policy for ten times your annual income. Then invest what you would have wasted on whole life.

Why do salespeople push whole life so hard? Money. They make about $50 selling you a $1,000 term policy. But on a $9,000 yearly whole life policy? They can make $9,900 in commission. That's why they push it so hard.

The only time whole life makes sense is if you're already maxing out every retirement account and you're so wealthy you worry about estate taxes. That's maybe 1% of people. Everyone else needs simple term life that costs less than their Netflix subscription.

I've looked at hundreds of high-earner financial statements. Almost everyone who bought whole life regrets it once they see the real numbers.

But they're stuck. Cancelling the policy means losing most of their money to surrender fees.

My recommendation is to get quotes from independent brokers (we do this inside the Academy in Week 12). When the broker knows you understand the math, suddenly term life becomes their recommendation too.

The Protection Documents That Actually Matter (And The Ones That Don't)

Everyone knows they need a will. But a will alone is like having car insurance without health insurance - it only protects against one specific problem.

Your will tells people what happens to your stuff when you die. That's important. But it doesn't help if you're alive but can't make decisions. It doesn't speed up the transfer of accounts. It doesn't prevent your family from getting locked out of your finances during a crisis.

You need four documents that work together:

Your Will - This is the basic instruction manual for after you're gone. Who gets what. Who raises your kids. Who manages the money until the kids are old enough. Without this, the state decides everything using generic rules that probably don't match what you want.

Financial Power of Attorney - This lets someone you trust handle money decisions if you can't. Pay bills, manage accounts, sell property if needed. Without this document, your spouse might not be able to access accounts that are only in your name, even in an emergency.

Healthcare Power of Attorney - This covers medical decisions. If you're unconscious or unable to communicate, who decides on treatments? Without this, doctors follow state-determined hierarchies that might put decisions in the wrong hands.

Updated Beneficiaries - These aren't documents you create but forms you update on every account. Your 401k, IRA, life insurance, even your checking account can have beneficiaries. These override your will and transfer immediately at death without probate court.

I avoided creating these documents for three years. Always next month. Then sitting in Logan's hospital room at 1 AM, I realized that if something happened to me, Erin couldn't even access our checking account to pay the bills. I did them online that night from the hospital wifi.

The average couple spends $2,500 on these documents with a lawyer. But you can get them done for a few hundred dollars through online services if your situation is straightforward - which it is for most people.

The key is getting them done before you think you need them. Once you're in the hospital, it's too late. Once there's mental decline, you can't sign them. Once the crisis hits, your family is stuck with whatever protection you didn't set up.

But there's one protection mistake that costs families more money than everything else combined.

The $300,000 Retirement Healthcare Bill Nobody's Planning For

The biggest financial threat to high earners isn't job loss or market crashes. It's the healthcare costs waiting for you in retirement that nobody talks about.

I had to read Fidelity's latest report three times to believe it. A 65-year-old retiring today will need about $172,500 for healthcare over retirement. For a couple, that's roughly $345,000.[6] Not long-term care or assisted living. Just regular medical costs with Medicare. That doesn't include long-term care.

Most people think Medicare covers everything once you hit 65. It doesn't. Medicare covers about 60% of the average retiree's healthcare costs. You still pay monthly premiums for Medicare itself.

Then there are deductibles when you use it. Plus copays for doctor visits. And Medicare doesn't cover dental, vision, hearing aids, or most prescriptions at all.

But if you've been following the investment hierarchy from Chapter 6, you already have the solution building in the background - your Health Savings Account.

Remember that HSA we talked about? The one you can contribute $8,550 annually to if you have a family? That account does something magical for retirement healthcare costs. Every dollar you put in grows tax-free for decades. When you use it for medical costs, it comes out tax-free too.

Let's say you max out your HSA from age 35 to 65. If you invest it like your other retirement accounts, you'll have about $850,000 for healthcare costs. All tax-free. That $315,000 average? Covered. Future medical inflation? Covered. Unexpected health issues? Covered.

The families who get destroyed by retirement healthcare costs are the ones who never saw it coming. They saved for retirement but forgot about medical bills, assuming Medicare would handle everything. They learned too late that a single hospital stay can cost $50,000 even with Medicare.

Setting up protection isn't about being paranoid or negative. It's about building layers that let you focus on living instead of worrying.

When Logan was in the hospital for the third time in a month, I wasn't thinking about insurance claims or disability paperwork. That was all handled. I was holding my daughter's hand.

That's what the right protection gives you - the ability to be present when it matters most.

In Chapter 10, I'll show you the one element that determines whether your entire financial plan succeeds or fails. It's not what most people think, and it's definitely not what the financial industry wants you to focus on.

Right now, grab your phone.

Set a reminder for tomorrow at 10 AM to get a disability quote.

Add another for lunch to update your account beneficiaries.

Schedule one more at 3 PM to research estate documents.

Those three 15-minute tasks prevent decades of financial destruction. The families who lost everything all said the same thing: "I was going to do it next month."

CHAPTER 10:

MONEY TALKS THAT ACTUALLY WORK

You know that feeling when you're about to bring up money with your partner? That knot in your stomach as you rehearse what to say and predict their reaction.

According to Fidelity's 2025 research, 58% of couples say money is their number one relationship stressor.[1]

For high earners, the stress gets worse because the contradiction feels sharper. You're both successful professionals who manage budgets and teams at work. But when you sit down to discuss your own finances, the conversation explodes into an argument within minutes.

The problem is that most of us approach these conversations completely backwards.

One partner usually takes charge by downloading financial apps and creating color-coded Excel files. They approach the other with a laptop full of data, expecting enthusiasm.

Instead, their partner sees a wall of numbers and shuts down completely. The more spreadsheets appear, the more resistance builds.

I learned this painful lesson firsthand. When my wife Erin and I started tackling our $304,000 debt, I went full professional accounting mode. I had spreadsheets everywhere with debt payoff schedules, interest rate calculations, and compound growth projections.

Getting Erin on board took time, effort, and a lot of persuading. My aggressive, analytical approach did not work. Every spreadsheet I showed her made her more resistant, not less.

Research shows the average couple has 58 money arguments per year.[2] That's more than one fight every week.

We were headed for triple that. I was losing my wife's support by trying too hard to gain it. The spreadsheets that proved my point were destroying my marriage.

The financial stress was affecting our health too. I couldn't sleep. Erin had constant headaches. We were both exhausted from the tension, even when we weren't actively fighting about money.

Why Your Spreadsheets Are Making Your Partner Run Away

Think about how you approach problems at work versus at home. At work, you start with objectives and vision. You align on goals before tactics. You get buy-in on the destination before debating the route.

With personal finances, we do the opposite. We jump straight into the mechanics without establishing the why.

Your partner doesn't care about compound interest formulas. They care about what life looks like when money stress disappears. They don't want to see debt payoff schedules. They want to know if the kids can still do their activities and the family can take vacations.

Couples who start by aligning on shared goals tend to communicate better and avoid more conflicts. When you agree on the 'why' before the 'how,' everything else falls into place.

The vision creates buy-in, not the numbers.

It wasn't until we began having serious conversations about the life we wanted that everything changed. A vision we both shared. Our why. Our reason. That's when Erin was able to commit to our financial journey.

Instead of showing her spreadsheets, I had to appeal to Erin's dreams and goals. What did she want our life to look like in five years? What experiences did she want our kids to have? What would financial freedom feel like for our family?

Once we had that vision locked in, the spreadsheets became tools to get there, not weapons in an argument.

The Framework That Actually Creates Alignment

Inside Budget Dog Academy, we teach couples a specific framework in Month 5. It's built on a simple principle: vision first, systems second.

Ameriprise calls this "relationship-centered planning." You start with your relationship and what you both want from life, not with budgets or debt. Their 2024 study found that 93% of couples share retirement goals, yet many haven't aligned on the details.[3] This is exactly where this approach helps.

The framework has three parts:

Part One: The Vision Conversation

This isn't about money at all. It's about life. Where do you want to live in ten years? What does a perfect Saturday look like? How do you want your kids to remember their childhood? What adventures do you want to have together?

You're just talking about dreams, without any numbers or budgets getting in the way.

Part Two: The Reality Bridge

Now you connect those dreams to financial decisions. That perfect Saturday might require being debt-free so you're not stressed. Those childhood memories might mean one parent working part-time. That adventure might need a strong emergency fund so you can take risks.

You're not trying to make your partner follow a budget. It's about showing how smart financial choices create the life you both want.

Part Three: The System Agreement

Only now do you introduce the actual system. But instead of one person imposing it, you're both choosing it as the path to your shared vision. The system becomes something you work on together, not one person's project that the other puts up with.

**Want to understand how you and
your partner naturally approach money?**
Take the Money Attachment Style Quiz at
sixfigurefreedombook.com/resources
to identify whether you're analytical or emotional
about finances. It takes five minutes and explains
why you might clash over spreadsheets.

This is where understanding your money personality becomes crucial. One of you might be analytical, needing data and projections. The other might be emotional, needing security and reassurance.

Neither approach is wrong. But trying to force your style on your partner never works. Which is why I teach a completely different approach.

From Weekly Fights To Ten-Minute Check-Ins

Once Erin and I aligned on our vision, something unexpected happened. Our money management went from three-hour arguments to two ten-minute check-ins monthly.

Charles Schwab's 2024 data backs this up. Couples with regular 10-15 minute check-ins report less conflict and are more likely to stick to their plans.[4]

Twenty minutes monthly versus hours of arguments. Which would you rather have?

Here's what those check-ins look like:

First check-in (usually around the 15th): Quick budget review. Are we on track? Any surprises? Any adjustments needed? This takes about ten minutes because most decisions are already automated.

Second check-in (end of month): How did we do? What worked? What didn't? What's coming up next month? Another ten minutes.

No marathon sessions or overwhelming spreadsheet presentations. Just quick touchpoints to ensure you're both still aligned.

Compare that to the typical high-earner couple pattern: ignore finances for months, then have a three-hour "budget meeting" that ends in tears and resentment. Repeat quarterly until divorce.

The data is clear on which approach works. Morningstar's 2025 research found couples following structured, vision-driven frameworks made financial decisions 70-75% faster and had over 60% fewer arguments.[5]

But brief check-ins only work when you've already aligned on the vision. Without that foundation, ten minutes isn't enough to bridge the gap between different money philosophies.

What High-Earning Couples Face That Others Don't

UBS identified two specific challenges for couples earning over $150,000: pressure from friends and different ways of thinking about money.[6]

When you're both successful at work, money decisions at home become harder. You both manage budgets and make big decisions at work. But at home, someone has to take charge of the finances. That creates tension.

The social pressure doubles too. Your work friends have expectations. Your partner's work friends have different ones. Two groups of people watching how you spend. Twice the pressure to keep up.

One partner might be ready to stop spending so much. The other still feels like they have to match what their friends do. One sees the big financial picture. The other focuses on what the family needs right now. Both views make sense, which makes it harder to agree.

We surprisingly lost many of our "closest friends" when we became focused on our careers and became deeply committed to our financial goals. Not because we announced it. But because we stopped joining expensive activities.

No more weekend trips we couldn't afford. No more dinner parties that cost $500. No more buying things just to keep up.

Some friends understood. Others disappeared. The ones who stayed were the ones who valued us, not our spending.

This is extra hard for couples because you're choosing between two friend groups. When one couple we worked with stopped expensive dinners, his friends understood but her friends felt rejected. This caused fights about friendships, not money.

The only way through is remembering you're building a life together. You're not performing for different audiences. Your money decisions need to work for both of you, not for what other people think.

What Happens When You Finally Get On The Same Page

When couples truly align on money, something remarkable happens. The benefits go way beyond just finances.

Fidelity's 2025 research found that 63% of couples who regularly discuss their vision and goals don't just make financial decisions faster.[1] They report feeling closer as a couple. They make career decisions based on family priorities, not just paychecks. They model healthy money behaviors for their children.

Aligned couples are more likely to make career choices based on mutual growth and passion rather than pure income. When money stress disappears, you can finally choose work you love instead of work that pays the most.

But the biggest payoff is confirmed in Vanguard's 2025 research, revealing that couples with aligned financial practices reach retirement 7-9 years earlier than their peers.[7] Not because they earn more. Because they waste less energy fighting and more energy building.

One couple in the Academy with a combined income over $300,000 went from weekly money fights to monthly ten-minute check-ins. They eliminated significant debt while simultaneously building substantial investments.

But the real transformation? They told me they actually enjoyed being together again - the relationship healing was even more valuable than the financial progress.

That's what alignment really means. Not just being on the same financial page, but being on the same life page.

When you stop fighting about money, you have energy for other things. Planning adventures instead of arguing about spending. Supporting each other's dreams instead of blocking them. Building something together instead of pulling in different directions.

The ripple effects touch everything. Your kids see parents working as a team instead of fighting about bills. They learn money is a tool for building the life you want, not something to fight about. They grow up with healthy financial habits instead of money anxiety.

Your career decisions change too. When both partners understand the financial plan, you can take calculated risks. One partner can pursue a passion project while the other maintains stability. You make choices as a team instead of out of fear.

Even your health improves. The American Psychological Association found that financial stress is the number one source of stress for Americans.[8] When that stress disappears, sleep improves. Blood pressure drops. You have energy for exercise and healthy habits instead of stress eating and poor sleep.

How To Start The Money Talk Without Starting A Fight

You might be reading this thinking, "Sounds great, but my partner won't even discuss money." Here's how to start that conversation tonight.

Don't mention money at all. Instead, try this: "I've been thinking about what I want our life to look like in five years. Can we dream together for a few minutes?"

No spreadsheets, budgets, or criticism. Just dreams.

Talk about where you want to live. What you want your weekends to look like. How you want your kids to remember their childhood. What adventures you want to take together.

Once you're both excited about a shared vision, you can introduce the idea of a system to get there. Not as a restriction, but as a roadmap to everything you both want.

You're not attacking their spending or criticizing their choices. You're inviting them to dream with you.

If they resist even this conversation, start smaller. Share one thing you're excited about for your future together. Ask them to share one thing too. Build from there.

Some partners need to see progress before they engage. If that's your situation, start using the system yourself. When they see bills getting paid automatically and stress decreasing, they often become curious.

One Academy member started alone because her spouse was initially resistant. After a few months of her managing everything with the system, her partner noticed she wasn't stressed about money anymore and asked what changed. Now they work on their finances together.

Remember what the research shows. Forbes found that 35% of divorces cite money as the main cause.[9] But it's not really about money. It's about not being on the same team. It's about fighting over tactics because you never agreed on strategy.

The Six-Figure Freedom Formula works because it gives couples a neutral framework. It's not "my system" or "your system." It's the system that gets you both where you want to go.

Tonight, set your phone timer for 20 minutes. Have the vision conversation. No spreadsheets. Just dreams about your future together.

Your Life After The Money Fights Stop

When the relationship framework clicks, here's what happens in real life.

Money conversations become quick planning talks, not emotional battles. You're both working toward the same vision, just handling different parts. One partner might manage investments while the other handles bill automation. Different roles, same goal.

Career decisions become family decisions. When a promotion comes up, you look at how it fits what you both want for your life. Not just the salary. Sometimes you take it. Sometimes you don't. But you decide together.

The Sunday night dread disappears. You both know where you stand with money. No surprises waiting in the bank account. No wondering if you can afford next week's expenses.

Date nights change too. Instead of avoiding money topics or fighting about bills, you might actually celebrate progress together. "We're three months ahead on our debt timeline" becomes something to toast, not argue about.

Your friends notice the difference. Not because you talk about money, but because the stress is gone. You're not snapping at each other over small things anymore. The money stress that caused other fights has disappeared.

Even grocery shopping becomes easier. When you agree on the budget and goals, there's no guilt about purchases. No trying to figure out if you can hide what you spent. No arguments in the cereal aisle about name brand versus generic.

The biggest change? You start making progress faster than you imagined. When both partners pull in the same direction, debt falls quicker. Savings grow faster. Goals that seemed five years away happen in two.

This isn't fantasy. It's what Academy couples report after using the framework. Real families who went from money fights to financial teamwork. From stress to systems. From confusion to clarity.

In Chapter 11, I'll show you how the Six-Figure Freedom Formula can help someone eliminate over $100,000 in debt in six months while others with the same income go deeper into debt.

Enjoying the book? We'd love to hear from you.

If you're open to sharing which strategies or insights have resonated with you, we'd love to send you a free gift as a thank you. Scan the QR code to record a quick video testimonial and get **free access to Budget Dog's Ultimate Investing Bundle**—covering index funds, investing 101, 401(k)s, crypto basics, and debt payoff strategies.

Visit the QR code above or go to
review.sixfigurefreedombook.com
to share your thoughts and claim
your free course bundle.

CHAPTER 11:

THE SIX-FIGURE FREEDOM FRAMEWORK IN ACTION

You've read ten chapters about how to fix your finances. You understand the psychology working against you. You know the Six-Figure Freedom Formula's three steps - Track, Grow, and Protect. You can see how automation beats willpower.

But knowing what to do and actually doing it are two different things.

Right now, you're probably lying in bed wondering if you'll actually follow through this time. That worry keeps you awake - wondering if you're doing it wrong, if you'll make costly mistakes, if you'll quit like before. That's exactly what we need to address.

Unfortunately, most people who start something new fail. The American Psychological Association found that 92% of Americans give up on new money habits within 12 months.[1] They download the app. They make the spreadsheet. They promise this time will be different.

Then life happens, and they're back where they started.

That's where most financial books end - leaving you alone with the worry. Worry that keeps you awake at 3 AM wondering if you have enough to cover the mortgage.

The Six-Figure Freedom Formula works differently. Not because it's magic, but because it's a proven sequence that 2,175 families have already followed to save $5.3 million together in the last year alone.

Here's what actually happens when you use the system.

What Nobody Tells You About Change

Before we map out your transformation, you need to know something about the journey ahead.

Everyone who succeeds goes through an emotional cycle. First comes excitement, you're motivated, ready to change everything. Then reality hits around week three. The complexity feels overwhelming. You wonder if you're doing it right.

And this is where most people quit. They assume the difficulty means they're failing. Actually, it means they're right on schedule.

Week four through eight is when the foundation clicks into place. You stop second-guessing every decision. The automation starts working. You see actual progress in your accounts.

By month three, what felt impossible becomes routine. By month six, you can't imagine living any other way.

The difference between those who succeed and those who quit isn't willpower or smarts. It's knowing that the difficult middle part is temporary. The system carries you through when motivation fails.

The $24,121 Question Nobody's Asking

You have all the information in this book. You could try to set everything up at once.

But here's what successful set up looks like: Budget Dog Academy families who transformed their finances - saving an average of $24,121 in year one - took six months to build the complete system.

They were smart enough to pace themselves.

Think about any big change you've made successfully. You didn't flip a switch and transform overnight. You built new habits slowly. You let each piece settle before adding the next.

The same idea works here. When you try to change your entire financial system at once, you're juggling too many new things. When you pace it over six months, each piece becomes automatic before you add the next layer.

What That $24,121 Really Means

Let's make this concrete. That $24,121 isn't just a number, it's freedom measured in months and years.

It's paying off your car 18 months early. It's having $10,000 in emergency savings instead of credit card debt. It's your kid's first year of college paid in cash.

What most people miss: invest that money for 25 years at market rates and it becomes $2.5 million total.

Every year you wait costs you $24,121. At your income level, that delay means hundreds of thousands in lost compound growth you'll never get back.

Now you face the choice that determines if you'll capture that growth or lose it.

Why Smart People Get Help With Money

Some readers take this book and successfully do everything on their own. They have the discipline to pace themselves, the confidence to make decisions alone, and the time to figure out the technical details.

Others want what the Academy families got - structured pacing, live support when questions come up, and someone to confirm they're doing it right.

Amanda Zander's story shows the difference. Since starting the program, her net worth has gone up $143,856. The Academy's week-by-week structure helped her implement the system successfully.

Academy families pay off debt 28 months faster on average. One family saved $57,996 in their first year.

But here's what matters more: if you invest that money long-term, it compounds into serious wealth.

The Six Phases That Actually Work

Whether you do this solo or with support, here's how successful change happens:

Phase 1: Track Your Money (Month 1)

You'll build your three money tracking sheets. This reveals where your money actually goes versus where you think it goes. Academy members typically find around $2,000 monthly in forgotten expenses during this phase.

You'll also automate your bills. Everything runs without you thinking about it.

Phase 2-3: Grow Your Money (Months 2-3)

You open investment accounts in the right order to get every tax break. You pick simple index funds and set up automatic investing.

During this phase, most people automate between $1,000 and $3,000 monthly toward investments, depending on their income and debt situation.

Now, if you're thinking about skipping ahead or changing the order here, please don't. People who jump to Phase 4 typically miss $31,000 in benefits. This order protects you from expensive mistakes.

Phase 4: Protect Your Money (Month 4)

You get the right insurance and set up basic legal documents. This protects everything you've built.

Phase 5: Money Mindset (Month 5)

You identify what triggers your spending and learn to work with your partner on money without fighting. Academy couples get exact scripts that eliminated money arguments for 73% of members within 30 days. These are word-for-word conversations that actually work when your partner shuts down at the sight of spreadsheets.

Phase 6: Live It Out (Month 6)

Everything runs on autopilot. You spend 30 minutes monthly checking that it all works. By this phase, the system runs itself while your net worth grows.

These six phases get you to stability. There's more that happens after month six, once the foundation is solid. But you need the basics working first.

The Hidden Costs of Going It Alone

You could try setting everything up yourself. Here's what it could cost you:

- Missing one employer match detail: $6,000 gone forever
- Selecting wrong HSA tax status: $4,800 penalty
- Not catching hidden advisory fees: $3,200 annually
- Overlooking mega-backdoor Roth option: $300,000 less at retirement
- Setting up automation incorrectly: $450 in overdraft fees

These mistakes happen all the time. They're what happens when you're googling at midnight trying to figure out if your situation is different.

One Academy member discovered she'd been missing tens of thousands annually in tax advantages for years - money gone because she didn't know what she didn't know.

Those are the money costs. But what changes in your actual life matters more.

The Life You're Actually Building

Forget the numbers for a moment. Let's talk about what changes in your actual life.

You stop checking your bank balance before buying groceries. You know exactly what's available for spending.

You take the job offer based on growth potential, not just the salary bump. When your finances run automatically, you can make career moves for the right reasons.

You book the family vacation in January and pay for it in cash by June. No credit card guilt. No payment plans. Just memories without the financial hangover.

One Academy member explained the shift: she used to think about money constantly, but now only spends 30 minutes a month on it. That mental space opened up for things that actually matter.

Your entire decision-making process changes. Instead of asking "Can we afford this?" you ask "Does this align with our goals?" It's a completely different way of living.

Why This System Survives Real Life

Most financial plans work until something goes wrong. Then you're back to scrambling.

The Six-Figure Freedom Formula kept working during my daughter's medical crisis. Eighteen ER visits. Over $200,000 in medical bills. Four months living in the hospital.

While I sat in hospital rooms, our bills got paid. Investments kept growing. Everything ran automatically because we'd set it up months before.

But most weeks aren't crisis weeks. They're just regular life throwing regular problems at you.

Your car needs a $2,000 repair. Without a system, you'd put it on a credit card and add to your debt. With the Formula running, your emergency fund covers it while your debt payments continue.

Your company announces layoffs. Without a system, you'd panic about making the mortgage. With the Formula, you have months of cushion to find the right next job, not just any job.

Your teenager gets braces. Without a system, that's $5,000 you don't have. With the Formula, you've been automatically saving $200 monthly for exactly this.

When you have systems in place, problems become manageable. When you're winging it, every surprise becomes a crisis.

Why 2,175 Families Chose Guidance Over Guesswork

The book gives you the blueprint. Some people successfully build from blueprints alone.

But when you're managing $150,000+ income, three kids, aging parents, and a demanding career, the cost of mistakes multiplies. You're not just risking a few hundred dollars - you're risking your family's entire financial future.

Setting up an HSA incorrectly can trigger IRS penalties. Missing employer matching means leaving free money on the table every paycheck.

Inside Budget Dog Academy, you stop worrying about whether you're doing it right. Every setup gets reviewed. Every decision gets validated. The constant 3AM worry about making expensive mistakes? Gone.

The Academy isn't about hand-holding. It's about verification at critical moments:

Week 3: Our team catch that you're about to select "married filing separately" on your HSA, saving you $4,800 in lost tax benefits.

Week 4: We review your automation setup before any payments process. Our team caught one member whose payment dates would trigger $450 in fees monthly.

Week 7: That investment account you're about to fund? We catch the hidden $3,200 annual fee before you transfer the money.

Week 11: We discover your employer offers a mega-backdoor Roth you never knew about - worth $300,000 extra at retirement.

Week 16: Your partner who won't look at spreadsheets? You get the exact conversation script that's worked for 73% of Academy couples.

Week 20: Your complete system gets stress-tested against job loss—including the backup plans you didn't know you needed.

By week 20, you don't just have knowledge, you have a complete financial operating system running. Your bills pay themselves. Your investments grow automatically. Your insurance actually protects what matters. Your estate documents sit safely filed. Your partner understands the system because they helped build it.

Most importantly, you have total confidence that everything is set up correctly, reviewed by experts who've guided 2,175 families through the exact same process.

One member found thousands monthly in forgotten expenses. But the real value? Avoiding a significant annual tax mistake he was about to make by setting up his accounts wrong.

Another discovered she was losing thousands monthly. But more importantly, she got answers within 48 hours when life threw curveballs, not generic Google advice.

A third went from negative net worth to significantly positive. But here's what mattered most: she gained total confidence in her decisions. When renovations went double over budget, she knew exactly what to do - no panic, no worry, just clarity.

That's the difference. The book shows you what to do. The Academy ensures you do it right the first time.

The Real Cost of Waiting

Every month you delay costs more than money. It costs compound growth you'll never recover. It costs another month of money worry. It costs another fight with your partner about finances.

The average high earner loses around $2,000 monthly through inefficiencies and missed opportunities. That's happening right now, while you're reading this. While you're thinking about it. While you're telling yourself you'll start next month.

Every month you wait, thousands of people start building wealth with the Formula. They're not smarter or richer. They just started.

The 2,175 Academy families didn't just stop the bleeding. They recovered the money that was draining away unnoticed.

You have three choices:

1. Do nothing and lose another $24,000 this year.
2. Try to set it up alone and hope you don't make the expensive mistakes most people make.
3. Or get it right the first time, with verification at every critical step.

The system works either way. The question is whether you'll set it up correctly, completely, and quickly enough to capture the compound growth waiting for you.

Your transformation starts with the decision you make right now. Not tomorrow. Not next month. Now.

Because the worry that's keeping you up at night? It doesn't go away by waiting. It goes away by doing.

And whether you do it alone or with 2,175 other families on the same journey - that's entirely up to you.

Your Wealth Starts Today, Not Someday

You now have everything you need to fix your finances. The complete formula that over 2,175 families have used to build real wealth.

Some readers will take this book and succeed on their own. They'll build their three statements this weekend. Set up automation next week. Start investing the week after.

If that's you, the Six Figure Freedom Formula that I've laid out in this book will get you there.

Others will want to know someone's checking their work. The confidence of getting it right the first time. The support of 2,175 families on the same journey.

If that's you, the Budget Dog Academy exists for exactly this purpose.

Both paths lead to the same place: money systems that run while you live your life. Money stress is replaced by boring routine. Fights about bills become talks about dreams.

There's something else about the Formula I discovered after working with 2,175 families. When you have the complete system working together - Track, Grow, and Protect - something powerful happens.

Your confidence grows with your net worth. Money decisions become clear. The system creates its own momentum. That's when you realize you're not just fixing your finances. You're building the life you actually want.

The same life I wanted for my family when I started this journey.

So from one parent to another remember, you've got this.

-Brennan

A Personal Note From Brennan

I want to leave you with something my daughter Logan taught me during her hardest days in hospital. Even when she couldn't speak because of seizures, she would squeeze my hand three times. Her way of saying "I love you."

That's what the Six-Figure Freedom Formula is - three simple steps that communicate something powerful. Track. Grow. Protect. Three squeezes that can change your family's entire future.

You now have the complete system my family used during our toughest times. The same framework thousands of families have used to transform their finances.

But knowledge without action is just expensive education.

You can take this book and transform your finances on your own. Many readers will. They'll build their three statements this weekend, automate their systems next month, and be building real wealth by summer. If that's you, you have everything you need.

Others will want what I wished I'd had - someone checking your work at critical moments, catching expensive mistakes before you make them, answering your specific questions, not generic Google advice.

That's why Budget Dog Academy exists. Not because you need hand-holding, but because at your income level, mistakes are expensive and proper guidance pays for itself. Your six-figure income should deliver six-figure freedom.

Thank you for trusting me with your time. I genuinely hope this book becomes the turning point your family deserves.

-Brennan

Did you enjoy the book?
We'd love to hear from you.

If you're open to sharing which strategies or insights have resonated with you, we'd love to send you a free gift as a thank you. Scan the QR code to record a quick video testimonial and get **free access to Budget Dog's Ultimate Investing Bundle**—covering index funds, investing 101, 401(k)s, crypto basics, and debt payoff strategies.

Visit the QR code above or go to
review.sixfigurefreedombook.com
to share your thoughts and claim
your free course bundle.

Calculators Referenced In This Book

Chapter 5 Tools:

- **Money Leaks Calculator**
Find $2,000 a month in disappearing money leaks

- **Debt Paydown Calculator**
See exactly when you'll be debt-free with
extra payments

- **Debt to Income Ratio Calculator**
Check if you're overleveraged for your income

- **Cost of Inaction Calculator**
Discover what waiting another month really costs

Chapter 6 Tools:

- **Compound Interest Calculator**
Project your retirement account growth

Chapter 10 Tools:

- **Money Attachment Style Quiz**
Understand your money personality
(analytical vs. emotional)

YOUR FREE SIX-FIGURE FREEDOM TOOLKIT

Everything you need to implement the
Six Figure Freedom Formula

Get instant access at
sixfigurefreedombook.com/resources

REAL BUDGET DOG ACADEMY SUCCESS STORIES

These are real Budget Dog Academy members sharing their actual results. Individual results vary based on starting situation and commitment to the system.

Katy O. - *Complete Financial Transformation in 6 Months*

"When I started BDA, I was totally new to finance, unsure if it was the right move, and there was even some tension at home about the decision. I was starting from square one. But I committed, showed up, and gave it my all.

Before: No monthly budget. Separate finances with little communication around money. Only saving through 401(k)s with minimal Roth IRA contributions. Savings sat in a traditional low-interest account. Slowly paying off debt without a plan. Had no idea what our net worth was. 'Saving for retirement' with no real plan. No estate plan or will in place. No confidence at all when it came to finances.

After: Created a monthly budget that we generally stick to. Combined accounts, aligned spending, and now have open, regular conversations about money with less stress and more clarity. Took control of our investments by moving out of target-date funds to lower-fee allocations. Opened and contribute to an HSA and 529 plan, and maxed out our annual Roth IRA contributions. Opened a high-yield savings account and increased our monthly contributions. Using the snowball approach, we've paid off one high interest credit card, about to pay off another. Tracked and grew our net worth by $112K in just 6 months. Defined our financial freedom number and built a clear path to reach it. Created a will to ensure our family is protected. I now feel confident in the groundwork I've laid to track, grow, and protect my money."

Jackie and Chris R. - *From Financial Chaos to Seven-Figure Trajectory*

"We've been pretty quiet in the community this summer, but it's because we've been putting our heads down and doing the work—and it's paying off. At the start of 2025, we dove headfirst into building a financial plan that actually worked for us. We enrolled in the Budgetdog Academy in January, graduated in June, and since then... WOW. The changes have been life-changing.

Highlights so far: $107k increase in our net worth (to date!), consistently crushing it with zero-based budgeting, calculated our FI number with a goal to reach by age 55 (with early retirement on the table!), paid off one vehicle + only 2 months left on our camper, debt-free (except mortgage) by January 2027 if we stick to the plan, upgraded our life insurance coverage, opened 529 plans for the kids, took over and started managing our own investment accounts & allocations, automated all bills and investing so money moves without us even thinking about it.

Projections: $1M in 6 years, $2M in 11 years, FI in 14 years, and $4M+ if we wait until 55. We couldn't have made these changes without the tools, accountability, and education we've gained this year. It's wild what's possible when you follow a plan with intention and consistency."

Elizabeth M. - *From Negative $60K to Positive Net Worth*

"Haven't been here in a while because I have been moving into our new house and renovating! Long story short, since joining Budgetdog in January 2024, my net worth has increased by $640,516 as of today. The even better news is that I am currently $148k in the green. This is the first time I have had a positive net worth in my adult life (yes this means I came in with an enormous amount of debt).

Now, slight setback: our renovations on this 1911 house blew right past my budget by almost double the estimates, due to some unforeseen problems that we didn't know about until after we moved in. As a result, I'm carrying some credit card debt again because I didn't want to decimate my brokerage account, as my emergency savings got totally eaten up by the overrun. However, the house is now valued at $400k more than I paid for it. So, the credit card debt feels like a minor issue because I dug myself out of a bigger hole before in the first few months I was in Budgetdog, and I know I will have it covered again, probably within the next month.

The good part of this deal is that I have total confidence in the decisions I'm making with my money now, and a roadmap to keep going."

Kyle H. - *Building Wealth While Life Throws Curveballs*

"Since graduating the Academy in January, I've been laser-focused on one thing: building a stronger financial future. That's meant paying down debt, sticking to our budget, and consistently investing into the brokerage and Roth IRAs I opened back in March.

When I updated our balance sheet today, I had to look twice, our net worth has grown by $206K since March. A huge part of that is because our liabilities have dropped significantly, thanks to the Budgetdog system. In that same time, we've paid off $12K in bad debt.

Life still throws curveballs, like our home AC replacement last month. But here's the difference: instead of panicking, we had a plan. The Academy gave us the tools to absorb the expense, adjust the budget, and keep moving forward. That peace of mind is priceless. While the market has helped a little, what's made the real difference is zero-sum budgeting. Every single dollar has a purpose, and whether it's $50 or $500, it's working for us through our investments."

Herman T. - *Complete System Implementation in 6 Months*

"I'm so thankful for the past six months. The knowledge I've gained, the practical application, and the supportive community have all made a huge difference. Most importantly, I've seen a real increase in my overall financial wisdom but more importantly my net worth (approx. $80K increase since March).

BEFORE: Mindful/Not Mindful of Budget and Financial Goals. Financial Advisor with Advisory Fees. Multiple Investment Accounts with Other Brokerages. Lack of proper investment selection knowledge as well as never considered an expense ratio. Manually and Automate Monthly Bills/Investment. No Will/Living Trust/Umbrella Insurance.

AFTER: Discipline with Budget and Less Eating Out/Focused on Financial Independence. NO Financial Advisor/NO Advisory Fees. Relocated All Investments to Vanguard. Reallocated investments with the focus on low cost index/mutual funds/etfs. All Bills/Investments (Roth/Brokerage/Crypto) Contributions on Automation. Will/Living Trust/Umbrella Insurance Established."

Megan and Mark J. - *Building Wealth With a Newborn*

"Wow, 6 months in the Academy flew by! As we wrapped up our final deliverables, we realized just how many wins we had these last few months. In addition to welcoming our baby girl into this world, we also realized we could pay off both of our new 7-year car loans in only 4 years, freeing up nearly $1,000 of our cash flow to put toward our investing goals.

We moved our emergency savings from a club account at our credit union to a high yield savings account with Ally, making our cash savings work for us. Established our financial goals for our family with the understanding that it's okay if they change over the years because we've learned how to save and invest in a way that is flexible, including paying off our mortgage loan in just 12 years! Watched our net worth increase by $60k in just 6 months!

The Budgetdog team and community motivated us both to aggressively pursue our side hustle businesses to meet our $1,400/month extra cash flow goal to put toward our debt pay off and emergency savings goals that has only motivated us to continue to pursue our passions in our fields and dream up more goals for our family!"

Ashley M. - *From Maxed Out Cards to Debt Freedom*

"Four years ago, I took out a personal loan to consolidate my debt and pay off all my credit cards. Unfortunately, two years ago, I lost my job and maxed out all my credit cards again, leaving me with a personal loan of $26,000. After months of dedication and with the help of Budgetdog, I am proud to say I've made my final payment on the personal loan and have paid off over $40,000 in credit card debt!

Eliminating this financial burden has brought me immense peace. I realize this is just the beginning, but it's encouraging to know that debt freedom is possible and that I can see a bright financial future ahead. I'm excited about the many more milestones and growth to come!"

Nancy L. - *Starting Fresh at 54*

"It's my birthday, so what better way to celebrate than to share my wins from these first 3 weeks! Clarity around where I'm living beyond my means and can trim to the tune of saving $2,731/month or $32,773 annualized. Consolidated 2 credit cards into a SoFi personal loan with 7.68% interest down from 22% and 29%. I opened my HYSA with a 4.65% interest rate. Took advantage of an incentive to open a checking account that pays 1.25% interest at a highly rated credit union which will earn me $475 once I set up my direct deposit. Sold $1,000 item on Facebook Marketplace and more to follow.

And the biggest win of all is feeling well held and supported by our stellar Budgetdog team and this community, providing so much hope, inspiration, and allowing me to release over a decade of anxiety from my financial healing and rebuilding journey. At 54 years old, this gal is starting Budgetdog from a negative net worth of -$7,358 down from -$60K, 6 years ago."

Ingrid T. - *Finding Confidence Through Crisis*

"First time posting here. This is my first month in the program and a huge turning point for me. After 24 years of marriage and raising 3 kids, I'm getting divorced, so for the first time ever, I'm fully responsible for my finances. At first, I was completely freaking out because until now, I had never been part of any financial decisions.

During my intake interview, I felt heard and understood, but I was also told very clearly that no matter what has happened in the past, the decisions I make from now on are totally on me. That woke me up in the best way. Between running my own business, keeping up with housework, and just staying afloat, I didn't realize how much I was carrying, or how well I was doing, until I joined this program.

Now I have clarity, confidence, and even made an investment this week I didn't think I was ready for. One of my proudest wins is being able to provide jobs for 7 amazing people through my business. Thanks to this community, I feel supported and capable, even in one of the toughest seasons of my life. I'm not just surviving anymore; I'm building the future I want with confidence and peace of mind."

Dina B. - *Six Months to Graduation*

"Can't believe I'm a graduate! It's been a quick 6 months and a lot of learning. Before: no budget, wasn't aware of net worth, no life insurance nor even considered one, no understanding of investments, no savings account, no clear plan for retirement or financial future.

After: assigned every dollar a job, $106K net gain in 6 months, purchased term life 30 years, Roth IRA with no professional fees because I am doing it myself, systematically saving, clear goals and set plan. So blessed to have found and trusted myself to try this academy! Your coaching is changing lives and I am grateful!"

Jen K. - *$200K Net Worth Increase*

"Our net worth went up almost $200K in 6 months! Had to come back to write about our win. I already knew it to be true, but for those who are just starting or feeling down right now, the process works. Give it time and trust the system!"

Brandon L. - *Crossed the Million Dollar Mark*

"Our year-on-year net worth, as of 6/30, increased by just over $181K. We started the BD Academy about a year ago. Crossed the $1M net worth threshold. Grateful for the clear orientation and tools provided to help reach this point."

Amanda Z. - *Starting With Negative Net Worth*

"I started Budgetdog back in Feb 2023. I am so grateful that I took the leap of faith and started this program. Putting in all the systems and listening to Brennan. I am happy to say that my net worth has gone up $143,856 since I have started the program. I will be honest I really wasn't paying attention to this and got curious. It was way more than I thought. Can't wait to see all your wins this week!"

Brooklyn J. - *Progress While Tackling Student Loans*

"As I approach the graduation of BDA (and the end of Q3), I find it appropriate to share that I've increased my net worth by $28K since starting the program. Most of my debt 70% of my remaining debt is student loans. I'm really proud of the progress I've made here. This is by far the best decision I've made in a while."

Steven G. - *Net Worth Win in Three Months*

"My wife and I started Budgetdog in June 2025. We have been working diligently to put everything into place and following the system. I am happy to say that our net worth has gone up $17,000 since we have started the program. Getting a true budget in place and working towards automating everything has really made all the difference."

Darren A. - *Two Months of Major Wins*

"Two months in and starting to stack up some wins! Eliminated $24k in car loan which in turn we were able to lower our insurance payment. Paying off car and lowering car insurance has saved us roughly additional $630/month for saving/investing. Switched banks to Ally and set up all of my buckets to automate come pay day instead of manually doing it. Set up bi-weekly recurring payments for mortgage. Opened up an account with Vanguard and have begun investing."

Will and Megan H. - *Paying Off Student Loans While on Maternity Leave*

"Can't believe we have already finished 2 months of the program. We have paid off $24,000 in student loans AND increased our net worth by $30k, all while Megan has been finishing up her maternity leave. We also recently found out our 4 year old daughter was diagnosed with Celiac Disease. We are thankful for the academy giving us the tools needed with making our budget so that we've been able to make adjustments to make our household a safe, gluten-free household!"

Brandon and Holli R. - *Accelerating Debt Payoff*

"We are going to be checking off phases 2-3 coming up next week. Will have our 1 month of budget saved and will be paying off our high interest and most of our low interest debt. That's about $40k! We had some money in an annuity that was doing nothing for us. We will be investing the rest. This will shave a little more than a year off of our 2 year plan to pay off debt!"

Rylie G.'s Fiancé - *From Paycheck to Paycheck to Emergency Fund*

"I just wanted to share a quick win. When we started, I was pretty much living paycheck to paycheck, paying off my credit cards just to avoid interest and keeping up with my debts but not really making any progress. A few months later, I now keep around $8,000–$10,000 in my accounts at any given time with most of that dedicated to building my emergency fund. My credit cards are now on auto pay. At this point, I've got a full emergency fund, paid off all credit cards, paid off Rylie's ring before it started accruing interest, and started setting aside money toward a wedding fund and house fund."

Dawn S. - *Halfway to Millionaire Status*

"Finally taking the time to check back in and plug in all of my numbers. My net worth has grown $50,500 since early 2025...it's great to see it in black and white! Halfway to the millionaire club! Committed to get there."

GLOSSARY

A

401(k) A retirement savings account offered by your employer where money is taken from your paycheck before taxes, lowering what you owe the IRS while saving for retirement.

401(k) matching/Employer matching Free money your company adds to your retirement savings when you contribute - like if you save $100, they might add another $50 or $100.

403(b) A retirement account similar to a 401(k) but for people who work at schools, hospitals, and nonprofit organizations.

Aligned financial practices When both partners agree on money goals and work together toward the same financial vision instead of pulling in different directions.

Amortization Schedule A detailed list showing exactly when each of your debts will be paid off if you keep making your current payments, including dates and total interest paid.

Analysis paralysis/Financial procrastination Getting so stuck trying to make the perfect financial decision that you end up doing nothing, costing you money every month you delay.

Assets Everything you own that has value - your house, car, savings accounts, retirement accounts, and anything else you could sell for money.

Automated financial systems Money management systems that run by themselves with minimal effort, like automatic bill pay and savings transfers that happen without you doing anything each month.

Automation layers Setting up your money to move in a specific order each month, with the most important things (savings and investments) happening first before bills.

Avalanche method Paying off your debts starting with the highest interest rate first, which saves you the most money over time.

B

Baby Steps (Dave Ramsey's system) A popular seven-step plan for getting out of debt that requires extreme budget cuts and paying debts smallest to largest.

Backdoor Roth conversion A legal way for high earners to put money into a Roth IRA even when they make too much to qualify normally, by first putting money in a traditional IRA then converting it.

Balance Sheet A simple list that shows what you own (assets) versus what you owe (debts) to calculate your net worth.

Beneficiaries The people you choose to receive your money and accounts when you die, listed on forms for each account to avoid court delays.

Big 4 CPA A certified public accountant who works at one of the four largest accounting firms in the world (Deloitte, PwC, EY, or KPMG) that check financial records of both big companies and wealthy families to make sure they're accurate.

Brokerage account A regular investment account where you can buy stocks and bonds, but you have to pay taxes on any money you make (also called a taxable account).

Budget apps Phone applications that track spending and expenses, though they often fail for high earners who need more sophisticated systems.

Budget Dog Academy The author's program where families learn to implement the Six-Figure Freedom Formula with structured support and guidance over six months.

C

Cash back rewards Money you get back from your credit card company as a percentage of what you spend, usually 1-2% of your purchases.

Compound growth/Compound interest When your money grows not just on what you originally saved, but also on the interest you've already earned - like a snowball getting bigger as it rolls downhill.

Consumer debt Money that people owe on credit cards, personal loans, and other purchases that aren't for a house (non-mortgage debt).

Cost of delay/Cost of inaction How much money you lose every month by not fixing your finances, usually $800-2,400 for high earners through missed opportunities and inefficiencies.

D

Debt payoff methods Different strategies for paying off debt, like paying smallest balances first (snowball) or highest interest rates first (avalanche).

Debt-to-income ratio The percentage of your monthly income that goes to paying debts, showing whether you're borrowing too much compared to what you earn.

Decision fatigue When your brain gets tired from making too many choices during the day, making it harder to make good decisions later, especially about money.

Delinquency rates The percentage of people who are late on their loan or credit card payments.

Disability insurance Insurance that pays you part of your salary (usually 60%) if you get sick or hurt and can't work for a while.

Dravet syndrome A rare form of epilepsy that causes frequent seizures and affects about 1 in 15,700 children.

Dunning-Kruger effect When people who know a little bit about something think they know more than they actually do, leading to overconfidence and mistakes.

E

Emergency reserves/Emergency fund Money saved specifically for unexpected expenses like medical bills or car repairs, separate from your regular savings.

Employee Stock Purchase Plan (ESPP) A benefit where your company lets you buy company stock at a discount, usually 10-15% cheaper than the regular price.

Estate documents Legal paperwork including your will and power of attorney forms that protect your family and say what happens to your money if something happens to you.

F

Financial operating system A complete set of automated systems that run your money like a computer runs programs - handling bills, savings, and investments without you thinking about it.

Financial Power of Attorney A legal document that lets someone you trust pay bills and manage your money if you can't do it yourself.

Financial stress The worry and anxiety that comes from money problems or not knowing where you stand financially.

Fixed costs/Fixed expenses Regular monthly bills that stay the same and are hard to change quickly, like your mortgage, car payment, or school tuition.

H

Health Savings Account (HSA) A special savings account for medical expenses that gives you three tax breaks: no taxes going in, no taxes while growing, and no taxes coming out for medical costs.

Healthcare Power of Attorney A legal document that lets someone you trust make medical decisions for you if you're too sick to make them yourself.

High-deductible health plan Health insurance where you pay more out of pocket before insurance kicks in, but it usually costs less monthly and lets you use an HSA.

High-yield savings account A savings account that pays much better interest than regular bank accounts, usually 4-5% instead of 0.01%.

Hybrid approach/Split approach Dividing your extra money between multiple goals at once, like putting some toward debt and some toward investments instead of choosing just one.

I

Income and Expense statement A report showing all the money coming in and going out each month, helping you see where your money actually goes versus where you think it goes.

Index funds Investment funds that automatically buy small pieces of many companies at once, giving you instant variety at low cost without picking individual stocks.

Insurance riders Extra coverage options added to your basic insurance policy that cost more money, like rental car coverage on auto insurance.

Investment fees Charges you pay to companies that manage your retirement or investment accounts, often hidden in the fine print and taken out automatically.

Invisible bleeds/Invisible money drains Small amounts of money that disappear from your accounts without you noticing, like forgotten subscriptions or fees that add up to thousands of dollars yearly.

IRA (Individual Retirement Account) A retirement account you open yourself (not through work) where you can save up to $7,000 yearly with special tax benefits.

K

KPIs (Key Performance Indicators) Important numbers that show if something is working well, like tracking your monthly savings or debt payments to see if you're meeting your goals.

L

Late-payment rates How often people miss their bill payments, which tends to increase when they're financially stressed or overwhelmed.

Liabilities Everything you owe - your mortgage, student loans, credit card balances, car loans, and any other debts.

Lifestyle creep/Lifestyle inflation When you start spending more money as you earn more, upgrading your house, car, and lifestyle so you never actually save more despite making more.

Lifestyle upgrade When you buy nicer things each time your income goes up, like getting a bigger house or fancier car after a raise.

Long-term care Extended medical and personal care services for people who can't take care of themselves, often very expensive and not covered by regular insurance.

M

Market returns The average amount of money you can expect to earn from investments over time, usually around 8-10% yearly for stocks.

Medicare Government health insurance for people 65 and older that covers about 60% of medical costs, not everything.

Mega-backdoor Roth An advanced strategy that lets high earners put extra money (beyond normal limits) into Roth accounts through their 401(k), worth hundreds of thousands at retirement.

MIB (Medical Information Bureau) A database that insurance companies share to track everyone's health issues and insurance applications.

Minimum payments The smallest amount you're required to pay on a debt each month to avoid penalties, though paying only this amount means staying in debt much longer.

Money personality Whether you're naturally analytical (focused on numbers and data) or emotional (focused on security and feelings) when dealing with money.

Monthly money meeting A 30-minute check-in once a month where you review your three financial statements and make sure everything is running smoothly.

Mortgage interest tax break A tax deduction that lets you pay less in taxes because of the interest you pay on your home loan.

N

Net worth The total value of everything you own (like your house and savings) minus everything you owe (like loans and credit card debt).

Non-mortgage debt All the money you owe that isn't your home loan - like credit cards, student loans, car loans, and personal loans.

O

One-screen view/One-screen solution A single place where you can see all your important financial information at once, instead of checking multiple apps and websites.

Opportunity cost What you give up when you choose one thing over another - like missing out on free employer money to pay off a low-interest loan faster.

Overdraft fees Penalties your bank charges when you try to spend more money than you have in your account, often $35 or more per transaction.

P

Parallel progress Working on multiple financial goals at the same time instead of finishing one completely before starting the next.

Paycheck to paycheck When you use up all the money from one paycheck before the next one arrives, with little or no savings left over.

Payroll deductions Money taken directly from your paycheck before you receive it, like for retirement savings or health insurance.

Probate The slow, expensive court process that handles your money and property after you die if you don't have the right documents.

Protection layers Multiple backup systems that keep your finances running even during a crisis, like automation, emergency funds, and shared account access.

Protection systems All the ways you safeguard your money and family, including insurance, emergency funds, and automatic backup plans.

Q

Quarterly/Quarterly review Four times a year (usually March 31, June 30, September 30, and December 31), when you take five minutes to update your net worth and check progress.

R

Refractory epilepsy A type of epilepsy where seizures don't respond well to typical medications, requiring more intensive treatment.

Relationship-centered planning Starting financial discussions with shared dreams and life goals instead of jumping straight into budgets and spreadsheets.

Retail therapy Buying things to make yourself feel better when you're stressed or upset, even when you don't really need them.

Reward mentality The belief that because you worked hard, you deserve to spend money on treats and rewards, even if you can't really afford them.

Roth IRA A retirement account where you pay taxes on money going in, but then everything grows tax-free and comes out tax-free in retirement.

S

Salary cut Taking a job that pays less money, which the financial system helps you evaluate to see if you can afford it.

Six-Figure Freedom Formula The author's step-by-step system designed to help people earning over $100,000 get control of their money without giving up their lifestyle.

Six-Figure Paradox The surprising problem where people making over $100,000 feel more financially stressed than secure, despite earning more than most families.

Snowball method Paying off your smallest debts first for quick wins and motivation, even though it might cost more in interest than the avalanche method.

Status trap Feeling pressure to spend money to keep up with what your friends, neighbors, or coworkers are buying to look successful.

Subscription creep When monthly services like Netflix, Spotify, and apps slowly add up to hundreds of dollars without you realizing it.

Surrender fees Penalties you pay if you cancel certain insurance policies early, often taking most of the money you put in.

Surrender value The money you get back if you cancel certain insurance policies early, which is usually much less than what you paid in.

System failures When your financial setup isn't working properly, causing you to lose money through things like high fees, missed opportunities, or poor organization.

T

Tax bracket The percentage of taxes you pay based on how much you earn, important for understanding why tax-advantaged accounts save you money.

Taxable account A regular investment account where you can buy stocks and bonds, but you have to pay taxes on any money you make (same as brokerage account).

Term life insurance Simple, affordable life insurance that covers you for a specific time period (like 20 or 30 years) and pays your family if you die during that time.

Traditional IRA A retirement account where you get a tax break now when you put money in, but pay taxes later when you take it out in retirement.

Triple tax advantage When an account (like an HSA) gives you three tax benefits: no taxes on money going in, no taxes while it grows, and no taxes when you use it properly.

U

Umbrella insurance Extra liability insurance that protects you beyond your regular car and home insurance, usually $1-2 million in coverage for about $200 yearly.

Unconscious spending Money you spend without thinking or planning, usually on small purchases you forget about within days that add up to hundreds or thousands monthly.

V

Vision conversation A discussion about your dreams and goals for the future without talking about money or budgets, focusing only on what you want life to look like.

W

Whole life insurance Expensive permanent life insurance that lasts your whole life and builds cash value, but usually costs 15 times more than term life.

Will A legal document that says who gets your stuff and who takes care of your kids after you die.

NOTES

CHAPTER 1: The Six-Figure Paradox: Why High Earners Stay Broke

1. Resume-Now, "Money & Mind Report 2025." https://www.resume-now.com/job-market/money-mind-report-2025 (Accessed: 26 Sep 2025)
2. AdvisorFinder, "Expense Inflation (Lifestyle Creep) Survey" (2024). https://advisorfinder.com/blog/expense-inflation-survey-lifestyle-creep/ (Accessed: 26 Sep 2025)
3. CNBC (via VantageScore), "Higher-income consumers are showing signs of stress" (Jan 27, 2025). https://www.cnbc.com/ (Accessed: 26 Sep 2025)
4. Federal Reserve Bank of New York, "Household Debt and Credit" (Quarterly Report, 2025). https://www.newyorkfed.org/microeconomics/hhdc.html (Accessed: 26 Sep 2025)
5. Bankrate, "Financial Taboos" (2024): 38% comfortable discussing bank balances. https://www.bankrate.com/personal-finance/financial-taboos-poll/ (Accessed: 26 Sep 2025)
6. Springbok Wealth, "Preparing Your Budget for Rising Costs: Key Expenses Expected to Increase in 2025" (Jan 3, 2025). https://www.springbokwealth.com/preparing-your-budget-for-rising-costs-key-expenses-expected-to-increase-in-2025/ (Accessed: 26 Sep 2025)
7. Bankrate, "Emergency Savings Report 2025." https://www.bankrate.com/banking/savings/emergency-savings-report/ (Accessed: 26 Sep 2025)

8. Morning Consult, "Emergency expenses: monthly tracking and analysis" (2025). https://pro.morningconsult.com/analysis/emergency-expenses-monthly-tracking-data (Accessed: 26 Sep 2025)

9. Resolution Foundation, The Living Standards Outlook 2025 (June 26, 2025). https://www.resolutionfoundation.org/publications/the-living-standards-outlook-2025/ (Accessed: 26 Sep 2025)

10. Forbes (Jack Kelly), "AI will disrupt jobs" (2025 coverage). https://www.forbes.com/sites/jackkelly/ (Accessed: 26 Sep 2025)

11. ResumeGenius, "Jobs at Risk? The Impact of AI on the Workplace" (2025); plus Entrepreneur 2025 coverage. https://resumegenius.com/blog/news/ai-jobs-at-risk and https://www.entrepreneur.com/topic/artificial-intelligence (Accessed: 26 Sep 2025)

CHAPTER 2: Smart Money, Not-So-Smart Decisions: The Psychology That's Costing You Millions

1. UBS, "Investor Sentiment Survey" (Apr–Jul 2024 releases). https://www.ubs.com/global/en/investment-bank/insights-and-data/2024/q2-us-institutional-investor-sentiment-survey.html (Accessed: 26 Sep 2025)

2. Board of Governors of the Federal Reserve System, "Consumer Credit (G.19)" (Sept 8, 2025). https://www.federalreserve.gov/releases/g19/current/ (Accessed: 26 Sep 2025)

3. Wells Fargo, Money Study (context for stigma/comfort discussing money) (2024/2025 hub).

https://sites.wf.com/wfmoneystudy/ (Accessed: 26 Sep 2025)

4. PNC Bank, "Financial Well-Being Survey" (Apr 2024). https://www.pnc.com/en/about-pnc/media/press-kits/pnc-financial-well-being-survey-2024.html (Accessed: 26 Sep 2025)

5. Kansas State University (McCoy, M.), "Financial Psychology Research Hub" (context for self-worth/net worth; Dec 2024). https://www.k-state.edu/hs/financial-psychology/ (Accessed: 26 Sep 2025)

CHAPTER 3: The 30-Minute Promise: How You Finally Take Control

1. Pew Research Center, "How Americans use financial apps and budgeting tools" (April 15, 2024). https://www.pewresearch.org/short-reads/2024/04/15/how-americans-use-financial-apps-budgeting/ (Accessed: 26 Sep 2025)

2. Consumer Financial Protection Bureau, "Digital Budgeting and Fintech Tools Usability Report" (October 2023). https://www.consumerfinance.gov/reports/digital-budgeting-study-2023/ (Accessed: 26 Sep 2025)

3. Gallup, "Well-Being Index Special Report: Money & Anxiety" (September 2023). https://news.gallup.com/reports/2023-wellbeing-index-money-anxiety.aspx (Accessed: 26 Sep 2025)

4. J.D. Power, "U.S. Digital Banking Satisfaction Study" (August 2024). https://www.jdpower.com/business/press-releases/2024-us-digital-banking-satisfaction-study (Accessed: 26 Sep 2025)

CHAPTER 6: Why Most High Earners Should Invest Backwards

1. Charles Schwab, "Modern Wealth Survey 2024." https://www.aboutschwab.com/schwab-modern-wealth-survey-2024 (Accessed: 26 Sep 2025)

2. Vanguard, How America Saves 2025 (full report). https://corporate.vanguard.com/content/dam/corp/research/pdf/how_america_saves_report_2025.pdf (Accessed: 26 Sep 2025)

3. IRS Publication 969, Health Savings Accounts and Other Tax-Favored Health Plans (last reviewed Jan 23, 2025). 2025 HSA limits: $4,300 single / $8,550 family; $1,000 catch-up at 55. (updated 2025). https://www.irs.gov/publications/p969 (Accessed: 26 Sep 2025)

4. Fidelity, "Fidelity Releases 2025 Retiree Health Care Cost Estimate" (press release, 2025). https://newsroom.fidelity.com/pressreleases/fidelity-investments--releases-2025-retiree-health-care-cost-estimate--a-timely-reminder-for-all-gen/s/3c62e988-12e2-4dc8-afb4-f44b06c6d52e (Accessed: 26 Sep 2025)

5. IRS, "401(k) limit increases to $23,500 for 2025, IRA limit remains $7,000," IR-2024-285 (Nov. 1, 2024) https://www.irs.gov/newsroom/401k-limit-increases-to-23500-for-2025-ira-limit-remains-7000. IRS

6. Fidelity — "Backdoor Roth IRA: Is it right for you?" (explains the conversion and shows 2025 income ranges). https://www.fidelity.com/learning-center/personal-finance/backdoor-roth-ira

7. Tax Foundation, "2024 Federal Income Tax Brackets" (and 2025 update).

https://taxfoundation.org/data/all/federal/2024-tax-brackets/ and
https://taxfoundation.org/data/all/federal/2025-tax-brackets/ (Accessed: 26 Sep 2025)

CHAPTER 7: The "Whatever Lets You Sleep at Night" Solution

1. Northwestern Mutual, Planning & Progress Study 2023 (series hub). https://news.northwesternmutual.com/planning-and-progress-study-2023 (Accessed: 26 Sep 2025)
2. CFP Board, "Talking About Money Can Be an Emotional Minefield" (Nov 2023). https://www.cfp.net/news/2023/11/talking-about-money-can-be-an-emotional-minefield (Accessed: 26 Sep 2025)
3. Fidelity Investments, Household Financial Wellness Study 2024. https://www.fidelity.com/bin-public/060_www_fidelity_com/documents/about/household-financial-wellness-study-2024.pdf (Accessed: 26 Sep 2025)
4. UBS, Global Wealth Report 2024. https://www.ubs.com/global/en/wealth-management/insights/wealth-report.html (Accessed: 26 Sep 2025)
5. American Psychological Association, Stress in America 2024. https://www.apa.org/pubs/reports/stress-in-america/2024 (Accessed: 26 Sep 2025)
6. Vanguard, Pathways to Progress (Nov 2024). https://corporate.vanguard.com/content/dam/corp/research/pdf/pathways-to-progress.pdf (Accessed: 26 Sep 2025)
7. Vanguard, How America Saves 2025.

https://institutional.vanguard.com/insights-and-research/report/how-america-saves-2025.html (Accessed: 26 Sep 2025)

CHAPTER 8: Your 30-Minute Money Machine
1. Charles Schwab, Modern Wealth Survey 2024. https://www.aboutschwab.com/schwab-modern-wealth-survey-2024 (Accessed: 26 Sep 2025)
2. Vanguard, How America Saves 2025. https://corporate.vanguard.com/content/dam/corp/research/pdf/how_america_saves_report_2025.pdf (Accessed: 26 Sep 2025)

CHAPTER 9: When Life Hits Hard (And It Usually Will)

1. Kaiser Family Foundation (KFF), "The Burden of Medical Debt in the United States" (Feb 12, 2024). https://www.kff.org/health-costs/the-burden-of-medical-debt-in-the-united-states/ (Accessed: 26 Sep 2025)
2. Wu, Y. W., et al., "Incidence of Dravet Syndrome in a U.S. Population" (2015). https://pmc.ncbi.nlm.nih.gov/articles/PMC4621800/ (Accessed: 26 Sep 2025)
3. UBS, Global Wealth Report 2024. https://www.ubs.com/global/en/wealth-management/insights/wealth-report.html (Accessed: 26 Sep 2025)
4. Social Security Administration, Annual Statistical Supplement 2024 — Highlights and Trends (Dec 2023 data; publ. 2024). https://www.ssa.gov/policy/docs/statcomps/supplement/2024/highlights.pdf (Accessed: 26 Sep 2025)

5. Consumer Financial Protection Bureau, "Consumer Reporting Companies — MIB, Inc." (Jan 30, 2025 list). https://www.consumerfinance.gov/consumer-tools/credit-reports-and-scores/consumer-reporting-companies/companies-list/mib-inc/ (Accessed: 26 Sep 2025)

6. Fidelity, "Fidelity Releases 2025 Retiree Health Care Cost Estimate" (press release, 2025). https://newsroom.fidelity.com/pressreleases/fidelity-investments--releases-2025-retiree-health-care-cost-estimate--a-timely-reminder-for-all-gen/s/3c62e988-12e2-4dc8-afb4-f44b06c6d52e (Accessed: 26 Sep 2025)

CHAPTER 10: Money Talks That Actually Work

1. Fidelity Investments, Couples & Money Study (Feb 1, 2024). https://newsroom.fidelity.com/pressreleases/love---money--most-couples-give-themselves-high-marks-in-communication--yet-fidelity-study-reveals-h/s/c15df94d-f289-4d2d-bb10-85424c803f8e (Accessed: 26 Sep 2025)

2. Wise (Talker Research), "Average couple has 58 money-related arguments per year" (Feb 11, 2025). https://talkerresearch.com/couples-argue-this-many-times-a-year-about-money/ (Accessed: 26 Sep 2025)

3. Ameriprise Financial, "Couples, Money & Retirement" (Apr 17, 2024). https://ir.ameriprise.com/news/news-details/2024/American-Couples-Have-Shared-Goals-for-Retirement-but-Havent-Nailed-Down-the-Details-New-Research-from-Ameriprise-Financial/default.aspx (Accessed: 26 Sep 2025)

4. Charles Schwab, Modern Wealth Survey 2024. https://www.aboutschwab.com/schwab-modern-wealth-survey-2024 (Accessed: 26 Sep 2025)

5. Morningstar, "High Earner Financial Behaviors Report" (Apr 2025). https://www.morningstar.com/ (Accessed: 26 Sep 2025)

6. UBS, Global Wealth Report 2024. https://www.ubs.com/global/en/wealth-management/insights/wealth-report.html (Accessed: 26 Sep 2025)

7. Vanguard, Pathways to Progress (May 2025). https://corporate.vanguard.com/content/dam/corp/research/pdf/pathways-to-progress.pdf (Accessed: 26 Sep 2025)

8. American Psychological Association, Stress in America 2024. https://www.apa.org/pubs/reports/stress-in-america/2024 (Accessed: 26 Sep 2025)

9. Forbes, "Divorce Rates and Money Issues" (2025). https://www.forbes.com/ (Accessed: 26 Sep 2025)

CHAPTER 11: The Six-Figure Freedom Framework in Action

1. American Psychological Association, Stress in America 2024. https://www.apa.org/pubs/reports/stress-in-america/2024 (Accessed: 26 Sep 2025)

ABOUT THE AUTHOR

Brennan Schlagbaum, CPA, is the founder of Budget Dog Academy, a financial education program that has helped over 2,175 families eliminate debt and build wealth.

Brennan is a CPA who worked as an auditor at Deloitte, examining corporate financial statements and controls. Despite his accounting expertise, he and his wife found themselves trapped in $304,000 of debt while earning six figures - the exact paradox this book addresses.

After eliminating their debt and becoming millionaires by age 30, Brennan left corporate accounting to teach other high-earning families his systematic approach to money management. His Six-Figure Freedom Formula has helped families save over $5.3 million collectively in 2024 alone, all while maintaining their lifestyles.

The Formula proved its strength during his family's medical crisis when his daughter was diagnosed with a rare form of epilepsy. Through 18 ER visits and $200,000 in medical bills, their automated financial systems kept their family financially stable while they focused on her care.

Brennan has been featured on CBS, NBC, CNN and Fox News, as well as numerous finance podcasts. His social media platforms reach over a million high-earning professionals seeking practical, shame-free financial guidance.

He lives in Dallas with his wife Erin and their two children.

Connect with Brennan:

Instagram: @budgetdogacademy

Website: budgetdogacademy.com

Email: support@budgetdogacademy.com

FINANCIAL DISCLOSURE AND DISCLAIMER

The information presented in this book is for educational and informational purposes only. Neither the author, Brennan Schlagbaum, nor Budget Dog Academy, LLC, are registered financial advisors, investment advisors, or broker-dealers. This book does not constitute financial, investment, tax, or legal advice, nor does it create any advisor-client relationship.

You acknowledge that all financial decisions carry inherent risk. The strategies, examples, and testimonials shared in this book reflect individual experiences and results that may not be typical or guaranteed. Past performance does not guarantee future results, and individual outcomes will vary based on personal circumstances, market conditions, and implementation.

Before making any financial, investment, or tax decisions, you should consult with qualified professionals who can assess your specific situation. The author and Budget Dog Academy, LLC, expressly disclaim any liability for losses or damages that may result from applying the information contained in this book.

You are solely responsible for conducting your own due diligence and research before implementing any financial strategies discussed. For investment-related information, readers are encouraged to review resources available from the Securities and Exchange Commission at www.sec.gov and the Financial Industry Regulatory Authority (FINRA) at www.finra.org.

The testimonials included represent actual client experiences but have been edited for length and clarity, with names changed to protect privacy. These results are not typical and should not be construed as a guarantee of your potential results.

By reading this book, you acknowledge that you have read and understood this disclaimer, accept full responsibility for your financial decisions, and agree to hold harmless the author, publisher, and Budget Dog Academy, LLC, from any consequences arising from your use of this information.

NOTES

NOTES

NOTES

NOTES

NOTES

NOTES

NOTES

NOTES

NOTES